On The Road To Freedom

A Pilgrimage In India

VOLUME II

Swami Paramatmananda Puri

Amrita Enterprises Private limited
Amritapuri, Kerala, India

ON THE ROAD TO FREEDOM
A Pilgrimage in India Volume II

written by Swami Paramatmanada Puri

Published by:
Amrita Books
Amrita Enterprises Private Limited Vallikavu
P.O., Kollam 690 525, Kerala, India

First Edition 2011, Second Edition 2014, Third Edition 2015, Fourth Edition 2019, Fifth Edition 2022, Sixth Edition 2024

Copyright © 2000 by Mata Amritanandamayi Mission Trust. All rights reserved. No part of this publication may be stored in a retrieval system, transmitted, reproduced, transcribed or translated into any language, in any form, by any means without the prior agreement and written permission of the publisher.

For more information contact:
Email: info@amritabooks.in
amritapublication@gmail.com

Website: www.amritabooks.com,
Ashram Website:
www.amritapuri.org
www.amritaworld.org
www.embracingtheworld.org
ISBN 978-93-88246-47-7

Dedication

This book is humbly dedicated to
Sri MATA AMRITANANDAMAYI
the Divine Mother Incarnate,
with deep devotion, respect and reverential salutations

gurucaraṇāmbuja nirbhara bhaktaḥ
saṁsārād acirād bhava muktaḥ |
sendriya mānasa niyamād evaṁ
drakṣyasi nijahṛdayasthaṁ devam | |

Completely devoted to the lotus-feet of the Guru, become released soon from the transmigratory process. Thus, through the discipline of sense and mind-control, behold the Deity that resides in your heart.

BHAJA GOVINDAM v.31

Introduction

It has been fourteen years since volume one of "On The Road To Freedom" was written at the suggestion of my spiritual Master, Amma, Mata Amritanandamayi. It was a personal account of the inner spiritual developments and outer journey that led to my meeting her. Volume one recounted how I became interested in spiritual life though leading a thoroughly material existence as a teenager in America, eventually taking me to Japan, Nepal and finally India. The first eleven years in India were spent in the company of various holy people, real saints and sages who had scaled the heights of spirituality. But in 1979, through the mysterious workings of Divine Grace, I was led to Amma who was in an entirely different category by herself. Here was a person who had attained a permanent union with God even at a young age. What was even more unusual was that she was utterly self-sacrificing, using her spiritual power to relieve the suffering of as many people as possible, initially from their worldly problems, but eventually leading them to spiritual realization and bliss. And Amma had and has the power to do it. Numbers are no limitation for her. I have seen her sit twelve hours at a stretch individually blessing twenty-five thousand people.

Introduction

The most amazing thing is that each one of those people seem to either be relieved of their suffering or undergo a deep change for the better in their inner lives. Amma knows what is needed by each person that comes before her. Her knowledge is intuitive and never-failing. And the peace and love that radiate from her are not of this world. Meeting and observing her, one comes to the conclusion that the Divine Amma truly exists and She really does care for Her children, this Creation.

The present book starts where the previous one left off. It is entirely about my life with Amma and contains many of her hitherto unpublished words. The first volume was felt by many to be a good introduction to Amma for those who have never met her. In this volume, I have tried to expose the reader to Amma's mysterious but grace-filled ways and enlightening teachings. If I have succeeded even slightly, it is solely due to her grace. All mistakes are mine while anything of value comes from her.

I am indebted to Swami Amritaswarupananda for his keen memory in recalling all the incidents of the liberation of the great devotee, Ottoor Unni Namboodiripad. May all of Amma's devotees bless me that I may get a little devotion to her lotus feet in this short lifetime.

In Amma's service,
Swami Paramatmananda Puri

Contents

Introduction 4

CHAPTER 1
Who is Amma? 9

CHAPTER 2
Days Before the ashram 25

CHAPTER 3
The Ashram is Born 55

CHAPTER 4
The First Disciples 66

CHAPTER 5
Amma as the Guru 85

CHAPTER 6
Faith Through Grace 143

CHAPTER 7
Going Abroad 165

CHAPTER 8
Computer Leela 197

CHAPTER 9
Brahmasthanam - Abode of the Absolute 209

CHAPTER 10
Tests of Faith 216

CHAPTER 11
Liberation of a Great Devotee 234

CHAPTER 12
The Vows of Renunciation 245

CHAPTER 13
"I Am Always With You" 258

Amma with Swami Paramatmananda - 1980

CHAPTER 1

Who Is Amma?

WHEN I FIRST CAME TO AMMA, I never suspected that she would become well known throughout India and the world. I thought that the few of us who lived with her in the little village of Vallickavu would be able to enjoy her company forever. Yet, as the years passed, Amma gave many hints about the future. One night, as I was walking through the ashram, my mind was struck by the extraordinary transformation of the present surroundings from the simple beginnings of the "good old days." What had started out as a small hut made of thatched coconut leaves with four of us living in it, had now become a huge complex of buildings accommodating hundreds of visitors. One day in the early years, as Amma and I sat in front of the meditation hall overlooking the yard, she turned to me and said, "The other day in my meditation, I saw that many rooms sprang up here, each one full of spiritual aspirants doing meditation."

"How is that possible, Amma?" I had interjected. "We have nothing with which to purchase land. Even if, by some miracle, we were able to acquire the land, with what could we build rooms?"

"Son, God has mysterious ways. If it is His Will, He will arrange it Himself. It is for us to abide by His Will and to do our duty."

Shortly after this, a devotee, in fact, purchased the land in front of the ashram and gave it to Amma. Soon, another devotee undertook to start a building which gradually evolved into the present temple and guest house of the ashram. Amma's words proved prophetic.

Because daily visitors were few in those days, Amma could sit out under the trees most of the time, meditating or talking in a leisurely way to the devotees. Today, with hundreds, even thousands of devotees regularly visiting the ashram from all parts of the world, Amma gives *darshan* at regular hours only. darshan is the time when she makes herself available to those who wish to see her and to hear their problems. At other times, it is difficult for her to stir from her room, for the moment she does, crowds of people flock around her to ask her for her blessings in their endeavors and to beg relief from sickness and distress.

Who is Amma?

Amma is revered all over the world as one of the few living and easily approachable saints established in *sahaja samadhi,* the natural state of abidance in the Transcendental Reality, the Self. The only word that can adequately describe Amma is "mysterious." One may live near her for many years and feel that one has understood everything about her, yet suddenly in her presence, one's mind may get confused and stunned at her unpredictable and mysterious ways, coming as they do from a transcendental source. Tradition says that only a Realized Soul can recognize a Realized Soul. After Self-Realization, one doesn't grow horns on one's head or bear any unique, distinguishing physical marks. Nor do sages walk around with signs hanging from their necks declaring, "I am a Liberated Soul," although some ordinary souls do! Just what ordinary people claim by being "liberated" is not clear; it is certainly not the state of freedom from identification with the body and mind. Otherwise, they would not need to make such a declaration. In the *Bhagavad Gita,* there is a conversation between Lord Sri Krishna and His devotee Arjuna, discussing just this point of how to recognize a sage. Arjuna asks:

> "What, O Kesava (a name of Krishna), is the mark of the man of steadfast Wisdom, steeped in samadhi

(the Supreme State)? How does such a one speak, sit and walk?"

The Lord replies:

"When, O Partha (a name of Arjuna) a man abandons all the desires of the heart and is satisfied in the Self by the Self, then he is said to be one stable in Wisdom. He whose mind is not perturbed by adversity, who does not crave for happiness, who is free from fondness, fear and anger, he is the sage of constant Wisdom. He who is unattached everywhere, who is not delighted at receiving good, nor dejected at coming by evil, is poised in Wisdom."

—Ch.2, v.54-57

It is presumptuous to try to label Amma since we do not share her state of Universal Love and Bliss. We are unable to show unflagging equal love to vast numbers of people as she does nor are we able to continuously sacrifice our time, health, sleep and comfort for the welfare of the world. We may, after a great investment of time and energy, be able to help in some small way one or two close friends or relatives. However, Amma transforms the lives of all whom she meets. She knows and understands the past, present and future of all who come before her and comforts and advises them in the light of that knowledge. Those who have sat near her for six or eight hours while she patiently gives *darshan* to ten or twenty thousand people know what I mean. It is something that has to be seen; it cannot be described. Even though it is difficult to understand Amma's state, there are ways by which we can conjecture who she is. In my life with Amma, I have seen and heard various things that convince me that the one we call Amma is the Divine Mother of the Universe, the Great Goddess Kali.

In the late 1970's and early '80's there was a *Mahatma* wandering around Kerala near Amma's village who was the first person to really understand who Amma was and who openly declared her to be the Divine Mother. His name was Prabhakara Siddha Yogi. He was an *avadhuta* (a sage who has transcended body-consciousness), and was therefore beyond following rules and customs set by man or religion. Avadhutas have attained God-Realization which is the fruit and purpose of all rules and scriptural injunctions. Yet they care for no one and spend their lives enjoying the Supreme Bliss of union with the Absolute Consciousness, which is their own Real Self. Such people may be taken for madmen or ghouls, or their behavior may be likened to that of an idiot or a child. But their actions have a deep inner significance which Amma says can be understood only by those on the same plane of Realization as themselves. In the ancient scriptures, there are many stories of such avadhutas, Jadabharata[1] and Dattatreya[2] being among the most well-known. In order to keep the public at a distance, they gave the appearance of being uncultured dullards, though they were really established in God. This *yogi* fit the description perfectly.

Prabhakara Siddha Yogi had been known in the area for more than a hundred years. The village elders used to recount stories to their children and grandchildren of his

---

[1] Jadabharata had been a king in his previous birth. He renounced his family and kingdom and went to a forest in northern Nepal to immerse himself in spiritual practice. He had attained a very high state but not full Self-Realization, when an untoward event happened that set him back spiritually.

While meditating, he heard a lion roar and opened his eyes to see a frightened and pregnant doe jumping across a stream. The fetus was dislodged and fell into the river and the mother deer died. Jadabharata took compassion on the fawn and rescued it and later raised it with great affection and care. Unfortunately, he became attached to it and in his last moments, instead of thinking of God, his only thought was of the deer. As a result, he was immediately reborn as a deer. In his deer birth, he remembered the incidents of his past life due to the good effects of his previous spirituality. He therefore left his mother and returned to his previous ashram and remained there thinking of God and awaiting his death.

In his next birth as the son of a brahmin, he also remembered everything. He acted like an idiot so that everyone would avoid him and in this way, he would not develop an attachment to anyone and be diverted from God-Realization.

[2] Dattatreya was the son of a sage and was considered to be one of the ancient incarnations of Lord Vishnu. He lived as an avadhuta and instructed famous kings of the day in spirituality. He is well known for his discourse to King Prahlada which compared twenty-four types of created beings to twenty-four different types of spiritual principles. He is said to be still alive and appears to his sincere devotees.

bizarre actions. His followers claimed that he was more than three hundred years old and said that they could prove it from old village government records. Whether or not that was true, there was no doubt about his strange and unpredictable behavior and the spiritual glow that surrounded him. Amma told us that he had many *siddhis* or supernatural powers. She spoke specifically about his habit of quitting one body and occupying another. In the *Patanjali Yoga Sutras*, this is called *parasarira pravesa siddhi* or the power of entering the body of another.

There is a classical story of a great renunciate or Hindu monk of ninth century India named Shankaracharya who had this siddhi or power. He was a Realized Soul who established the supremacy of Advaita Vedanta or the philosophy of Non-duality which teaches that what exists is only the One Reality called *Brahman*, the Absolute, and it is That which appears as God, the world and the individual soul. That is our Real Self or True Nature. He wrote elaborate commentaries on the *Bhagavad Gita*, *Upanishads* and *Brahma Sutras*, in addition to numerous devotional hymns to God, all before the age of thirty two, at which time he sat in samadhi and left his mortal coil. During his travels around ancient India, he would debate with the greatest scholars of each place in order to prove the truth of Advaita. One day, he was challenged by a scholarly woman to a debate on the science of eroticism. Being celibate from birth, he had no knowledge of the subject and therefore asked for one month's time in order to prepare his debate. To this the woman agreed.

Being a world teacher and *sannyasi* (monk), Shankaracharya had no intention of bringing a bad name to his life's calling and therefore came upon an alternative expedient. Having found out that the local king had just died, he entrusted his body to his disciples' care and going into a yogic trance, he then left his own body and entered the body of the king. Naturally, everyone was surprised to see the king come back to life, but they were nonetheless delighted to have him back, especially the queens. In this "new" body, Shankaracharya indulged in sexual pleasures and gained the knowledge he required. Interestingly enough, the queens and the courtiers noticed that the king had become unusually intelligent, much more so than before his death, and they therefore came to the conclusion that a great yogi had entered the dead body of their king. Not wanting to lose him, they sent messengers all over the countryside with orders to cremate the body of any dead monk they find so that the soul inhabiting the king's body would have nowhere to go. Fortunately, Shankaracharya discovered their designs and returned to his own body just in time. He then defeated the woman in the debate with his newly acquired knowledge.

Similarly, Prabhakara Siddha Yogi enjoyed living as an avadhuta on this earth and did not want to waste time between births or in growing up after each birth, and so, when one body became old and weak, he would just leave it, entering into another "ready-made" one! He had moved like this in and out of many bodies. Hearing about him, Amma had a desire to see such a being and therefore simply thought of him. The next day he arrived at her house.

"Did you call me here?" he inquired.

"Yes. How did you know?" Amma asked him.

"I saw an effulgent light on my mental screen yesterday and understood that you wanted to see me, and so I have come," he said.

Now this avadhuta had a very bad reputation for troubling women. Stripping off his clothes, he would run after them and try to catch them, regardless of the consequences. When he was criticized for this, he said, "What do I care for earthly ladies? At all times I am surrounded by a bevy of celestial damsels worshipping me! Is it my fault if you can't see them?" One day he said to his followers, "I am feeling a little bit of ego in my body. I think something should be done to get rid of it." He then went to a nearby village, inquired where the Superintendent of Police lived, and went to his house. After knocking on the front door, he stood there waiting. Finally, the wife of the policeman came to the door. The avadhuta immediately caught her in a bear hug! Of course, this did not go over very well with her husband, who took hold of him and beat him up to his heart's content. He then locked him up and had one of his arms broken. Mysteriously, the yogi disappeared from the jail the next day and was found in another place, sound in all limbs. Because of such conduct, whenever he entered a village, the women locked themselves behind closed doors and the men folk beat him or chased him away. If the reader wonders why a yogi should act in this manner, Amma would say that only those in his state can know! The explanation cannot be understood from the ordinary person's viewpoint. He is not identified with a body and is totally detached from this world. His viewpoint is quite inconceivable for us who are still asleep in this dream of illusion (*maya*).

True to his nature, the yogi tried to catch hold of Amma, who was in her early twenties at the time. She immediately caught his hand in an iron grip and said, "Don't you know who I am? I knew your father, your grandfather and your great grandfather!"

"Oh, yes, You are the Divine Mother Kali Herself.

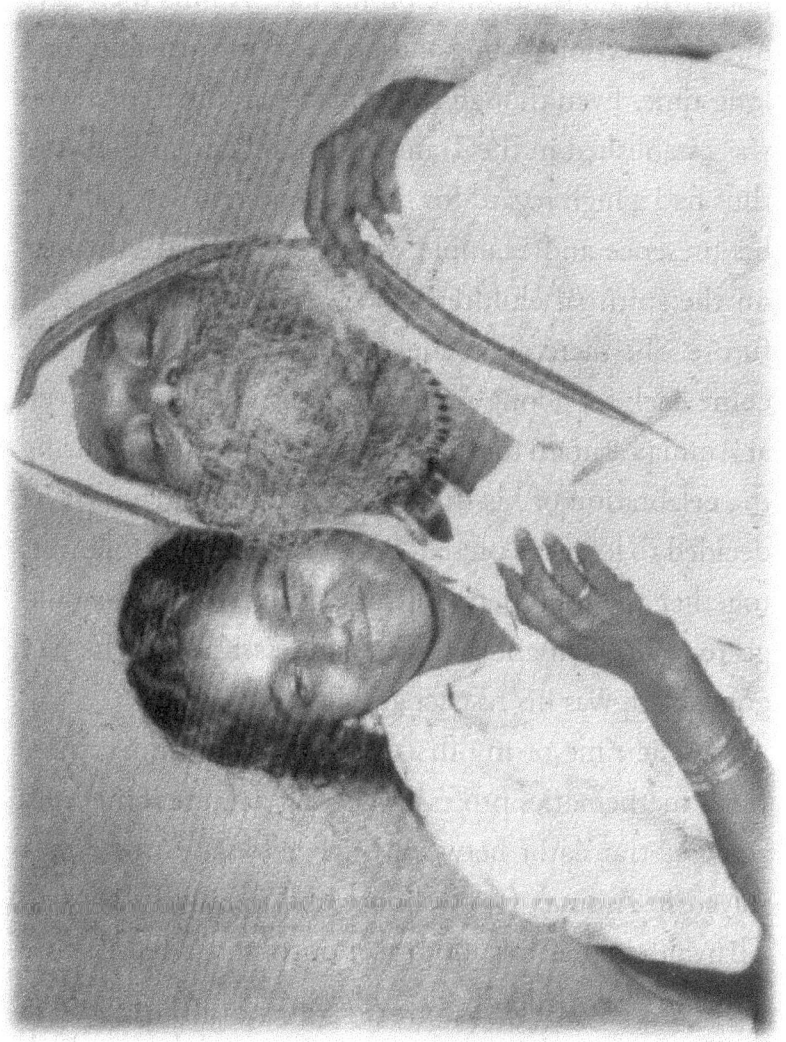

Amma with Prabhakara Siddha Yogi

In the future, people will come from all corners of the earth to this holy place for Your darshan!" the yogi replied with a blissful smile on his face. Amma then gave him an affectionate hug and he went into samadhi for a long time. Even though she considered him as one who was established in the Transcendental State of Bliss and thus had a high regard for him, she nonetheless felt that his presence and example would exert a bad influence on the spiritual children who were to come to her in future. She therefore made a resolve that he should not come back for a long time, and in fact, he was not seen at Amma's ashram for many years to come. It was during the celebration of his three-hundredth birthday that he decided to leave his present body. He called his followers together and told them only one thing: that they should go to Vallickavu and tell the Goddess Kali that he had gone. Such was his respect and love for Amma.

At the time of my first meeting with Amma, there was a mathematics professor visiting her. He sometimes acted as translator between us. For four or five days I stayed in Amma's family house and then went back to Tiruvannamalai for about a month and a half before returning permanently to Vallickavu. During the time in Tiruvannamalai, I had a dream one night in which I found myself sitting in Amma's temple during Devi

Bhava. She smiled at me and, pointing to the person sitting next to me, asked if I knew him. I replied that I did not. Amma mentioned that the person sitting there had good detachment and devotion. After this, I woke up. I called to the friend who was staying with me at the time and asked him to make a note of the dream in his diary, indicating the date and time. I thought that perhaps something might have occurred at Vallickavu for which I would want accurate verification later.

After three days, I received a letter from the mathematician who wrote: "Sunday I went to Vallickavu and had Amma's darshan. During the Devi Bhava, I sat next to Amma and requested her to give you darshan in Tiruvannamalai. Asking me to take the trident which she sometimes holds during the Bhava darshan, she said that she would give you darshan. It was midnight at the time. Did you have any experience then?" It was, in fact, Sunday at midnight that I had seen Amma in Devi Bhava in my dream! The same man had a vivid dream a few days later. He dreamt that Amma appeared to him and told him to make me understand that she was the Divine Mother incarnate.

Amma once had the following conversation with some devotees. Though humorous and characteristically without ego, her words nonetheless indicate who she really is.

Amma: Even before Creation, Lord Shiva had related what was inevitable. And even afterward, He gave the necessary instructions about how one should live here in this world.

Question: What do you mean, Amma?

Amma: Before Creation, Shakti (the Primordial Nature, Cosmic Energy) heard a voice saying, "There is only sorrow in creation; You should not undertake it." It was the voice of Shiva (Pure Consciousness). Shakti replied, "No, it needs to be done." Thus even before Creation, Shiva had given hints to Shakti regarding the nature of Creation. It was only after the warning that He granted permission to create.

After Creation, He, the Pure Consciousness aspect, receded. In reality, He has nothing to do with all these things happening around us. Later, Shakti ran to Him, complaining, "I have no peace. Look here, the children are scolding Me. They blame Me for everything. Nobody takes care of Me."

Shiva said, "Didn't I tell you that it was going to be like this and that you should not pursue it (Creation)? Now you create an uproar, having gone ahead. Aren't you the one who is responsible for all this having happened?

There was no problem when I was alone, was there?"

Amma: Sometimes here in the ashram when the children's longing for God declines, Amma cannot bear it. She feels inexpressible pain. At these times, Amma tells her children, "Alas! Shiva told me not to depart from Him and bother with all this. Look here, now I am suffering." (All burst into laughter.) Now how can I go complain to Him? He will ask, "Didn't I warn you about this earlier?"

I remember when some devotees asked Amma about her realization of the Truth. In those days, Amma used to call herself a "crazy girl" who knows nothing. However, on this occasion she was more explicit about herself. She said, "Amma has never felt that she is different from her real Infinite Nature. There was no time when she was not That. The so-called knowing, or realizing moment or time, was only a rediscovering, to set an example, removing the cover. There is no time when an Avatar is not aware of His or Her true nature. An Avatar is Consciousness embodied with all It's splendor, glory and fullness.

"Space is there before you build the house. Space still exists even after the completion of the house. The only difference is that now the house is in space—it exists in space. The house occupies a little space in the vast space. Space continues to be even after the demolition of the house. The house comes and goes but space remains in all three periods of time, the past, present and future. Rediscovering one's own true nature by removing the veil is applicable only to a soul who evolves stage by stage to the state of Supreme Consciousness. But this is not applicable to an Avatar. An Avatar is like space. He or She always lives in that Consciousness. There is no knowing or realizing in Their case. They are eternally That."

CHAPTER 2

Days Before the ashram

THE ASHRAM HAS NOT ALWAYS been so peaceful as it is today. Shortly after Gayatri (Swamini Amritaprana) and I arrived from Tiruvannamalai to settle near Amma in January of 1980, someone tried to poison Amma during Krishna Bhava because of old jealousies of the villagers towards her. I had heard of attempts made on her life, but this occurrence took place with myself as an eyewitness.

At the end of Krishna Bhava, Amma would always drink a little milk brought by the devotees. Lord Krishna, after all, had been famous for His love of dairy products, especially milk and butter. Amma became terribly sick after drinking some of this milk one night. Although she finished the Krishna Bhava, she began vomiting repeatedly afterwards. Inspite of that, she began the Devi Bhava shortly after the Krishna Bhava as was her usual way. Before going into the temple, the devotees pleaded with her to take rest and cancel the darshan. To this, she replied,

"Children, most of the people who have come for darshan are very poor. A good number of them are laborers who work for daily wages. It is by saving ten to twenty cents each day that they are able to save enough money to visit Amma once a month. They have little understanding of what spirituality is; they come to Amma for a little solace, to hear a kind, consoling word. If they are asked to come back, they will have to wait another month before they can afford to pay a second visit. Also, there are a few devotees, hailing from distant places, who come for darshan perhaps only once or twice a year. They would be very upset if the darshan is discontinued; to give them sorrow for the sake of my own comfort is unthinkable. Let Amma carry on with the darshan as far as possible. Then, if Amma collapses, it has to be accepted as the will of God."

Amma sat for the Devi Bhava, but the doors of the temple had to be closed repeatedly while Amma was vomiting inside. Being inside with her, it was very painful for me to watch this suffering that she was going through for the sake of the devotees. At last, the darshan was over. As Gayatri was prostrating to Amma, Amma fell off her seat on to the ground and the doors were then closed.

Amma then revealed the truth of the whole episode. She said that at the end of Krishna Bhava, a devotee had

offered her some milk according to the custom. In this case, however, the milk had been poisoned by the person who had sold the milk to the devotee. Amma said that the milk vendor was an atheist who was against Amma, and when he heard that the milk was going to be offered to her during Krlshna Bhava, he poisoned it. Completely unaware of this, the woman had offered it to her. She said that she had known all about the milk being poisoned when she saw it. Taken aback, we asked her why she drank it. She said,

"When the devotee offered Amma the milk, Amma didn't accept it at first, knowing that it was poisoned. The devotee became very upset because of this and began to wail. She was innocent. Feeling pity for her, Amma then drank the milk. The devotees bring offerings with great expectations and if Amma were to refuse them, they would be very grieved. So Amma had to drink the milk regardless of the poison. Don't worry, children. Amma will soon be all right." Amma then went to the house and laid down exhausted and in great pain. Bhaskaran, a great devotee of the Divine Mother who lived nearby, sat with Amma the entire night, chanting the stories of the Goddess until sunrise. What a voice! Even without understanding the words, I could feel his devotion. From the quality of his voice, one could tell he was truly a master bard.

Bhaskaran looked upon Amma as his own daughter during her ordinary mood and as a vessel of Lord Krishna and of the Divine Mother, respectfully, during the Bhavas. Over the years, he had many wonderful experiences through Amma's grace. In order to make a living, he used to travel from village to village singing the Srimad Bhagavatam and other scriptures, accepting whatever money was offered for his services. He had heard about Amma's Krishna Bhava and came a few times, but he was not thoroughly convinced that who he was seeing was Krishna Himself. One night, he had a vivid dream. Krishna appeared to him and said, "Son, you have been roaming around from village to village, holding Me (Srimad Bhagavatam) under your arm for so many years and what have you gained? Here I am right under your nose in Krishna Nada (Amma's house) and you do not recognize Me. How foolish you are!" Bhaskaran woke up, startled. From then on, he regularly came to Krishna Bhava. One day on his way back from a nearby village, he passed by a pond which belonged to a temple and was attracted by the lotus flowers growing there. He thought, "How nice it would be if I could offer one of these to Krishna." Going to the priest of the temple, he expressed his desire, and after obtaining permission, plucked one of the flowers and started on his way to Amma's place.

Along the way, a charming little boy stopped him and begged him for the flower. Bhaskaran was in a dilemma. He felt an inexplicable attraction to the boy and was inclined to give the flower to make him happy, but at the same time, he felt that it was wrong to give something which had been intended for God's worship to a human being. Finally his heart won over his sense of duty, and he gave the flower to the boy. When he reached the ashram, Amma was already standing in Krishna Bhava. As soon as he entered the temple, she called him over to her side and smilingly asked, "Where is the flower?" Bhaskaran's heart jumped; he could not say a word. Then Amma affectionately patted him on the head and said, "Don't worry, that little boy to whom you gave the flower was Me, Krishna."

One night near the end of Devi Bhava, Bhaskaran was sitting outside the temple. Amma called him inside, blessed him and gave him a stick of burning incense. She then told him to go home immediately. It was only ten o'clock and Amma finished the Devi Bhava shortly afterwards. This was highly unusual, for even when the crowds were small, the darshan would continue at least until one or two in the morning. After the darshan, while we were sitting around Amma, she said, "Tonight one of my children is going to die." We all looked at each other, slightly apprehensive. "Who is that, Amma?" we asked. But Amma did not reply. We went into the hut and lay down to rest. Suddenly we heard pitiful wailing coming from the other side of the village. Amma immediately got up and stood outside, intently looking in the direction of Bhaskaran's house. Then she called us and we all walked over there. As soon as we entered the house, Bhaskaran's wife stopped crying and told her children also to be silent since Amma had come. Such was her respect for Amma, that even in that extremely painful situation, she insisted on proper respect being shown to her. Bhaskaran's body lay lifeless on a mat on the floor. Amma asked how his end came. His wife said, "He came home, had his meal and lay down, saying that he felt a little pain in his chest. Immediately after that he was gone." We all sat there for some time and then followed Amma back to the ashram. On the way we asked her, "Amma, what was his fate after death?" "Where could he go but to the world of the Goddess?" replied Amma with a slight smile illumining her face.

In those days, at the beginning of the Devi Bhava, Amma used to come out of the temple and dance in ecstasy, holding a sword and a trident. She really looked like the fierce form of the Goddess Kali, with her tongue hanging out and a roar issuing from her mouth. Sometimes she would be so ecstatic that she would roll on the ground letting out peals of laughter all the time. Seeing Amma in that mood, we felt that we hadn't understood her at all. It was during this time that we had to be especially careful about the way we played music. It had to have exactly the correct beat and tune.

One night during Amma's dance, I made a mistake while playing the harmonium, a small instrument like a pump organ. Amma ran over to me and came down on the harmonium with her sword. Seeing the sword sweeping down, I immediately pulled my hand away and fortunately so, for she took a big gash out of the instrument just where, the moment before, my hand had been. The person next to me who was playing the tabla or drum, also made a mistake in the beat and down came the sword a second time, cutting off the head of the drum! We were naturally frightened and a little upset. We avoided Amma the rest of the night, thinking that she was angry with us. However, after the darshan, she said to us in a loving tone:

"Whatever be my mood, I am always your Amma. There is no reason to be afraid. I was not angry at you for my own sake but rather for the sake of the subtle beings who were enjoying the music."

"What do you mean, Amma?" we asked.

"During the dance, many beings come to see me in that mood. I see them as tiny dots of pulsating light. Their whole being gets absorbed, as it were, in the beat and tune of the music. When you make a mistake, it is a terrible shock to their whole system. Just imagine if you were blissfully absorbed in a beautiful tune and suddenly the musicians started to play off key. How would you feel? It would be very painful, wouldn't it? That is why, seeing their pain, I got angry with you."

At this point, a discussion about the subtle planes of existence might be apropos. Just as we have a physical body made of flesh, bones, and nerves, a subtler body made of thoughts and feelings called the mind, and a causal body in which the mind merges in deep sleep, God also has these different bodies, but on a universal scale. Both Amma and the ancient scriptures of India point out that this universe is only the grossest manifestation of the Cosmic Being's Universal Body. There are many other planes of existence that we cannot see with our physical eyes that are populated by an infinite number of living souls. It is from there that we have come before birth and it is to there that we will go after leaving the physical body at death. As Lord Krishna says in the Bhagavad Gita:

> "O Partha, neither in this world nor in the next is there destruction for him; none verily, who does

good, My son, ever comes to grief. Having attained to the worlds of the righteous and having dwelt there for eternal years, he who failed in Yoga is reborn in a house of the pure and wealthy. Else, he is born in a family of wise yogis only. Verily, a birth like this is very hard to obtain in this world. There he gains touch with the knowledge that was acquired in the former body and strives more than before for perfection, O son of the Kurus."

—Ch.6, v.40-43

One whose consciousness has become subtle and unmoving through prolonged spiritual discipline can see these subtle worlds. Both benign and harmful beings exist there just as they do here. They have varying degrees of spiritual power as do people here on earth. All donuts may look alike on the outside, but inside some have custard, others have jam and still others, chocolate. Similarly, the inner stuff or subtle body of living beings varies according to their spiritual evolution. All are created equal only in the sense that the spark of divinity, consciousness, and life are the same in all. Other than this, everything else differs from soul to soul.

In the beginning days of the ashram, a large number of people used to come to Amma to be rid of possession by subtle beings. Some of these beings are in a painful emotional state. They may also be extremely hungry or thirsty and unable to satisfy their urges. They therefore await an opportunity to somehow interface with beings on the physical plane of existence so as to get some relief from their suffering. In attempting to be rid of them, most people engage "ghost-doctors" or "white magicians" who know various *mantras* which will chase these beings away.

Just before I came to Amma, I had known a girl who was possessed by a very powerful subtle being. She and her poor family had been living in a rented apartment, part of a house in which there were other tenants as well. One of the neighbors felt compassion for this family and built a little house, giving it to them as a present. Unfortunately, one of the tenants of the apartment felt jealous towards them for their good luck and decided to kill the father of the family using black magic. He went along with the black magician to their house and knocked on the door, but it was the girl who came to the door instead of her father. As soon as she opened the door, she felt a tremendous force hit her and she fell on the ground. From that day onwards, she had a feeling of inner emptiness which gradually developed into hearing a male voice within her. Whenever anyone would come near her with the intention of getting rid of this possession, the evil spirit would start to ring her insides like a wet towel, causing her to scream so loud that people could hear her cries a mile away.

The evil spirit eventually told her that he had been a virtuous *brahmin* in his previous life and had been practicing meditation on the side of a holy river while living in a hut. One day someone visited him and left a book on black magic for him to read. At first, he was not interested, but then, curiosity got the better of him. He read it and started to experiment to see whether he could actually control forces in the subtle plane through the prescribed mantras. His experiments ultimately led to the destruction of many hapless victims and of himself as well. The girl's family had tried everything to get rid of the possession but had failed. One day, the girl heard another voice telling her that it was her family's Guru speaking and that he would save her if her mother would vow to fast indefinitely until the evil spirit had been vanquished. This was told to the mother who started to subsist on water and lemon juice. Eventually, the mother became so weak that she died, leaving the father and grandmother to look after the girl who was by this time completely bedridden. The voice had obviously been the deceitful evil spirit.

Feeling very sorry for this family, I narrated their whole

history to Amma and asked her if she could do anything to help them. She replied,

"Ask them to come here. No evil spirit is as powerful as the Goddess. Surely she will be relieved."

I conveyed Amma's words to this family through a letter, but I never received a reply. Moving the girl was all but impossible, as the evil being would start to torture her even more. What a terrible fate! Perhaps she had died by the time my letter reached them.

One night a man who was having a lot of physical problems came to the ashram during Devi Bhava. He had been to a number of doctors over the past few weeks, but none could help him. He finally heard about Amma, the refuge of the helpless, and came to see her. I was standing inside the temple at that time and overheard Amma asking him whether someone in his family had recently died of a snake bite. He replied that, indeed, his brother had died of a cobra bite just a few weeks before. Amma asked if the funeral rites had been performed, and found that, for some reason, the man had not performed the prescribed rites and rituals for the deceased. She told him that his physical problems were due to the fact that his brother was troubling him, trying to draw attention to his plight in the other world, for he desired the rites for the deceased. Amma then asked the man to sit on the ground in front of her. She threw a large quantity of flowers in the air above the man's head, all the while smiling and looking in the air above him. I kept staring at the same place, but I could not, of course, see anything. The man left after Amma had done this ritual worship. We later heard that he was rid of his problem.

On another Bhava darshan day, I was sitting next to Amma when a devotee came for darshan. As he put his head on Amma's lap, his body shook a little. Amma looked over at me with a smile on her face and made a sign with her hand like a snake with its hood expanded. Abruptly, the man jumped up and started to roll on the ground. He crawled out of the temple on his back and immediately crawled back in. He was lying on his back, his eyes looking towards the door of the temple away from Amma. She motioned with her hand that he should go out of the temple. Though he could not have possibly seen her wave her hand, he immediately crawled out of the temple on his back. After a while, he returned in his normal mood. Amma later told me that he was regularly possessed by a *naga*, a subtle being somehow related to the cobra family on this plane of existence. They become very displeased when cobras are killed and will cause trouble to those who do so. For Amma, all planes of existence are visible, and she is neither surprised nor frightened by anything that takes place in any of them. She sees everything as her own Self in different forms, like a dreamer sees a dream as the projection of his own mind.

In the early 1960's, a very unusual phenomena took place in a little village in Andhra Pradesh, one of the Indian states. A villager had been walking through the fields, when he came upon a white cobra in the middle of the path. He had never seen or heard of a cobra of that color and thought that perhaps it was a supernatural being in that form, equating it with the god Subrahmaniam, the son of Lord Shiva. He placed his upper garment on the ground in front of the snake and prayed, "If you are Lord Subramaniam, please get on this cloth and I will take you to a temple." Much to his surprise, the snake got onto the cloth and sat docilely there while he carried it to the Shiva temple in the village. After setting it down, the man stood by and watched as the snake slithered into the pond adjoining the temple, had its bath and then headed for the inner shrine. It first circled the Ganesh image and then coiled around the Shiva *lingam*, holding its hood erect.

Hearing about this, many people from the surrounding villages flocked there to see the wonder snake. As the days went by, the snake did not eat anything. Finally, someone came up with the idea of worshipping it. As part of the worship, a cup of milk was offered to the snake. As soon as the appropriate mantras were repeated, the snake bent down and drank all of the milk! From that time onwards, the snake became the "pet god" of the village, allowing itself to be worshipped, fed, fondled and petted even by young children. Every day it would bathe in the pond and after circling the other deities in the temple, would come and take its place on the lingam. Thousands of people started to come to that remote village which necessitated the building of a road, initiating public bus service and installation of electricity by the government. Many saints came to have the darshan of the holy snake. While one such mahatma was sitting in front of the temple singing to the accompaniment of a harmonium, the snake crawled out of the inner shrine, climbed up on the harmonium and then slithered over the sage's arms, around his neck, and then down to the ground and back into the temple, leaving the swami in ecstasy. This swami was a personal friend of mine who related the incident to me with great emotion.

Feeling jealous of the prosperity of the temple, a rogue eventually caught hold of the snake while no one was around and killed it. He then captured an ordinary cobra and, stitching its mouth closed, set it on the lingam.

Days Before the Ashram

When he came back a few hours later to see what was happening, the snake had somehow loosened the stitches and bit him. He soon died a miserable death. Having gone to that village and seen the photos of the miraculous snake being petted and worshipped by children, I was not surprised when various incidents related to snake divinities used to occasionally take place around Amma. Surely there are planes of existence unseen by our gross vision.

Once, during one of Amma's dances during the Devi Bhava, a man came with the intention of doing some mischief. Amma stepped out of the temple, holding the sword and trident in her hands, and started dancing in the open space in front of the temple. The man grabbed the sword, trying to pull it out of Amma's hand. Although he did not succeed in getting the sword, he hurt Amma's hand. Immediately, the entire crowd fell upon him and gave him the beating of his life. Seeing all this violence going on, my body started to shake, yet Amma could not have possibly seen me in that condition, for she was dancing in another part of the compound. I was surprised when the darshan was over, and she looked at me and laughing, said, "Why were you shaking so much when that fellow tried to hurt me? Because he received immediate punishment for his misdeed, he need not suffer afterwards."

Some time after this, there was another attack on the ashram. It was at the conclusion of the Krishna Bhava. Amma was intoxicated with bliss as we all chanted the divine names of the Lord. She gave one last loving glance to her devotees, and then stepped back into the temple, the doors gently closing behind her. The music came to an end, and the whole scene gradually became still. Everyone was standing in silent prayer, immersed in devotion to Amma as Krishna.

Suddenly a rough looking man who was standing in front of Gayatri started shouting something. He appeared to be somewhat drunk. Rallying around their leader's cry, a few other ruffians came forward from the back of the crowd and surrounded Amma's father, Sugunanandan. They began shoving him back and forth, knocking his glasses off. Sugunanandan became furious, shouting at them to leave the property. Suddenly, the leader of the gang pulled out what appeared to be a deadly home-made weapon: a belt with heavy metal hooks attached to one end. It looked like he was about to hit Amma's father with it. Gayatri quickly dashed forward and ripped the belt out of his hands, running fast to escape the hoodlums' wrath. Several devotees sprang forward to protect her from the bullies, and within moments, a brawl ensued. Gayatri somehow managed to escape from the thick of the fight, and quickly ran and closed the latch on the temple door, locking Amma inside, fearing that She would come out and be attacked by one of the ruffians. Balu and Sreekumar had run inside to protect her and I was already in there to assist Amma at the end of the darshan. There were terrible noises outside surrounding the temple—shouting, screaming and the sound of things being torn down. Inside the temple, Amma was roaring, "Kali! Kali!!" trying to get out, but we would not let her. We had to forcibly hold her inside lest some rowdy should harm her. Slipping around to the back of the temple, Gayatri hid the weapon in a stack of old boards and quickly returned to stand guard at the temple door. Within a minute, half the youths in the village had converged on the spot, ready for a brawl. The devotees, usually a peaceful lot, were now proving themselves willing to do battle for Amma's sake, and before long, about fifty men were fighting it out to the accompaniment of the anxious cries of the women. It looked like a scene out of the Mahabharata War.

No one really had any idea what was happening or why. After twenty minutes or so, the fight somehow subsided and the villagers began to disperse. Although many devotees and family members had sustained minor injuries, to our relief, no one had been seriously hurt.

When Gayatri opened the temple doors, Amma came rushing out, expressing concern for anyone who had been injured. She lovingly caressed those with bruises and black eyes, which included a few of her own relatives. She then addressed the group.

"Children, many of the local people are very hostile to Amma and are looking for some way or other to destroy Amma and the ashram. Due to their ignorance and jealousy, the youths from about twenty houses joined together tonight in a hateful scheme to attack Amma's relatives and kill Amma. About two weeks ago, Amma warned Sugunanandan about the possibility of such an attack, advising him not to remain outdoors for too long. She also advised him to avoid picking quarrels with anybody, because Amma felt that the people were looking for provocation."

Amma turned to Sugunanandan, and said with great love, "Even if people abuse you, you should learn to maintain your peace and equanimity. We have surrendered ourselves to the Supreme Self. Therefore, we should learn to see everyone as God in all circumstances. We should learn to accept praise and abuse with the same detachment." Sugunanandan seemed a bit astonished, replying, "But a couple of those scoundrels were here in the morning saying they were hungry—and we gave them money!

Days Before the Ashram

Yet tonight they returned to beat us!" Amma answered, "They are only displaying their nature. No matter how they behave, we should adhere to our *dharma*, and try to see the Divine Oneness within all."

Amma again addressed the devotees. "Children, we should look upon this event as an opportunity to study our own minds. We should not over-react or start jumping at shadows. Our actions should not depend on the words which come out of these hoodlums' mouths. The diamonds of peace we have obtained through our *sadhana* cannot be forfeited for peanuts. Spiritual life is meant to break the shell of the ego that covers our Self, not cultivate it. In difficult circumstances like these, great faith and patience are required. God is our protector. If we rely on Him alone, He will take care of us. If we catch hold of the queen bee, all the other bees in the hive will serve and protect us."

"Children, we must all be very careful now. We should try to avoid circumstances in which we are likely to lose our balance. Let us keep our hearts open and trust in God. If we try to conquer their ignorance by force, they will only come again with greater vengeance. Remember, children, hatred never ceases through hatred, but only through Love."

Having comforted the devotees, Amma then went

back into the temple to begin the Devi Bhava. To many of us, Amma seemed even more compassionate than usual that night, as if expressing her appreciation for the courage the devotees had displayed.

Naturally, this brawl immediately became the prime topic of conversation among the villagers and rumors abounded. We soon learned that many people were laying all the blame on Amma. It seemed like a good time to stay within the ashram grounds and avoid the village completely if possible. In those days, even in ordinary circumstances, some of the villagers would seize every opportunity they could get to harass Amma. Whenever she would pass by their houses, they would tell their children to hoot at her and pelt her with stones. To prevent this, the disciples asked Amma to avoid taking long walks through the streets, but she wouldn't agree.

Seeing all of this, I wondered whether I really wanted to stay in Vallickavu forever. This was no ashram—it was a battleground! Was I ready to die here amidst the fighting? I finally decided that there was really no choice in the matter, that I could not "chicken out" and abandon Amma. As the Bhagavad Gita says, it is better to die doing your own duty than to live doing the duty of another. Fortunately, this fight was the last of such violent incidents. Yet my appreciation for Amma's fearlessness continued to increase as more of her life was revealed to me. This uproar was just a fraction of what used to go on when the "Committee of a Thousand" had formed to destroy Amma in the old days before I had come. She stood all alone by herself; even her family did not protect her. Yet she was dauntless in the face of continuous harassment. The Committee, a group of over a thousand young men from the coastal area, banded together out of various motives of self-interest and general rowdiness. They tried diverse means to either expose her as a fraud or to kill her, but in every case they failed miserably. Many of the Committee members eventually became Amma's most ardent devotees as a result of experiencing her divine and benevolent powers. One of the leaders actually married one of Amma's sisters later on.

Just imagine if you were a teenage girl in Amma's position. Even if you were surrounded by loving friends and relatives, if there was a threat to your life, you would become fearful. Yet, for Amma, there was no one in this world. What could be the explanation for her unique dauntlessness in the face of such overwhelming circumstances? Her natural abidance in the state of conscious Oneness with God and her knowledge and experience that this seemingly substantial world and the body that lives in it are nothing more than an illusory dream projected on the indestructible screen of Awareness—only this can account for her remarkable courage. There is no other explanation possible. Some people, after they come to spiritual life, begin claiming their identity with God, yet could any one of these pretenders remain fearless in similar circumstances? The proof of the pudding is in the eating.

In my early days in Vallickavu, I could not speak Amma's language, Malayalam. Fortunately, Balu (Swami Amritaswarupananda), Sreekumar (Swami Purnamritananda) and a devoted householder named Krishna Shenoy used to regularly come and they could all speak fluent English. Mr. Shenoy has written many moving devotional songs appealing to Amma for her grace to save him in his difficulties. Sometimes devotees wake up with a bang to their eternal relationship with Amma.

As Amma says, "Remember that all those who are associated with Amma in this lifetime were also with Her in their previous births. You can see only this lifetime and therefore think you did not know Amma before. But you have all been with Amma before. No one remembers or knows his connection to Amma in previous lives. There is a predestined time for each one to come to Amma. Some come earlier, others later. But every one of Amma's children has always been with her. They come to Amma at different times, sometimes when they hear about her or when they see her photograph. Other times, it happens when they listen to a recording of Amma's *bhajans* (songs). In some cases people come to her after meeting one of her children; still others realize their relationship to Amma only through direct contact with her.

"Some talk about 'before meeting Amma,' but there is no such thing. All of Amma's children have already met Her long ago. Even though no one is aware of this, Amma's protection has always been there with them."

Shenoy's first meeting with Amma had totally changed his life. When he was in his mid-forties, he was a hardcore Communist. His entire family wanted to go and see Amma one day and insisted upon his accompanying them. In a weak moment, he agreed and they all came to Vallickavu on a Bhava darshan day. Arriving before the darshan had started, they sat under a tree near the temple. Nearby, there was a group of teen-age girls who were talking and playing. They were all similarly dressed in colored skirts and shirts, and all of them appeared to be girls from the village. Suddenly, Mr. Shenoy felt an overwhelming force pulling him towards one of the girls. Like one in a trance, he walked over to the group of girls. Falling down, he placed his head on the lap of one of them and burst into tears like a baby. He lay there crying for a long time, and finally when he sat up totally stunned, the girl looked at him with a smile on her face and said, "Child, I was expecting you to come. Now you have nothing more to worry about. I will always be with you." Again Mr. Shenoy burst into tears and finally getting up, went and sat by the tree as before. His family members asked him, "Have you been here before?" He replied, "I have never even been in this area before. This is the first time I have ever come here."

"Then how did you know which one of those girls was Amma? There is nothing which indicates her as any different from the others."

Mr. Shenoy answered, "I don't have the slightest idea what happened or how it happened." Just imagine what would have happened if that girl had not been Amma!

A great transformation took place in Mr. Shenoy after this. He completely severed the connection with his Communist friends, and became a committee member for the local temple near his house. This temple was in a bad state of disrepair and the devotees decided to construct a new temple for the nagas, a deity depicted as having a snake's body with a human head. They removed the sacred images to a nearby spot and built the new temple. The night before the consecration of the temple, Mr. Shenoy came to Vallickavu to get Amma's blessings and to invite her to the ceremony. He entered the temple during Devi Bhava. Seeing him, Amma said,

"I know why you have come. Don't worry. Everything will happen smoothly, and I will go ahead of you and make my presence felt at the new temple."

Mr. Shenoy immediately returned to his village by the first available bus. Proceeding to the temple, he found all of the committee members gathered excitedly at the entrance to the temple compound. He wondered why they were not busy with the ceremonial preparations and asked them what was the matter. They replied,

"About an hour ago, a cobra came here, slithered around the naga images and then entered the temple. We followed it with a flashlight but could not find it anywhere. There is no way that it could have come out of the temple without our seeing it, and now there is a strong smell of jasmine flowers inside the sanctum sanctorum."

After the ceremonies, Krishna Shenoy went back to Amma's ashram. Before he could say anything, Amma said to him, "I hope you are satisfied with my appearance at the temple. I got there quite a while before you and then came back." Needless to say, Mr. Shenoy's devotion became unshakable after this, and in due course, he came to settle at the ashram.

One morning, as we were all sitting around Amma, Sarasamma, a lady devotee of Amma's who was living in a village about eight miles from the ashram, came running up and fell onto Amma's lap, crying hysterically. Amma just sat there with a blissful smile on her face. Sarasamma finally composed herself a little and sat up and tried to speak, but her words were stuck in her throat. Some time passed before she began narrating a most interesting experience that had happened to her the previous day.

She said, "I left the ashram around four o'clock in the morning with my son Madhu, and we boarded the bus in Vallickavu. It was pitch dark when we reached our village around five. I got out at the stop which I thought was just near my house and thought that my son was getting off by the other door of the bus. Immediately after I stepped out, the conductor rang the bell, and the bus drove away into the darkness. Looking around, I could not find my son, and I soon realized that I was at a lonely place about two kilometers from my house. My son later told me that upon turning around in his seat, he was shocked to not find me on the bus. Alighting at the next bus stop, he started to run back to where I was, which was quite a distance away.

"Perplexed and not knowing what to do, I remembered Amma's parting words, 'Be very careful today.' I tightly

Days Before the Ashram

held Amma's *prasad* (usually food or flowers that have been blessed) in my right hand. I saw a truck stop a short distance up the road. Seven or eight men emerged and walked towards me. Perhaps they had seen a lone woman alighting from the bus in this forlorn place. Surrounded by these burly-looking rowdies, I was quivering with fear as they shot questions one after another towards me, using vulgar language. I thought that they might attack me at any moment. A terrible fire raged within me. 'Is this the fate of those who go to see the Holy Mother? Is this the fruit of my life-long devotion?' Such thoughts burned within me, making me oblivious of the surroundings and I shouted at the top of my voice, 'Amma!' This shocked the rowdies who surrounded me.

"What followed is difficult to express. Suddenly and unexpectedly, the effulgent form of the Divine Mother appeared before me in the sky with countless arms, holding various weapons in Her hands. She was seated on an enormous creature, and Her face, hair and crown resembled exactly those of Amma during Devi Bhava. Amma had assumed the terrible form of Kali in order to save her devotee! Realizing this, I started to lose my external awareness. The Divine Mother stretched out Her arms towards me. Gazing at Her radiant form, my eyes became transfixed and they started to bulge. As my tongue began to stick out like Mother Kali's, I felt a tremendous power pervade my body and an appalling laughter burst out from me, the mere remembrance of which sends shivers down my spine. The air trembled with the ghastly sound of that laughter. The rowdies, who were about to pounce on me, were taken aback upon seeing this frightening form roaring with laughter, standing before them fearlessly with disheveled hair, bulging eyes, and protruding tongue. Perhaps they thought that I was an evil spirit instead of a human being! Losing all their courage, they altered their course and retreated, slowly backing up. Scurrying into the truck, they drove away posthaste.

"Even after their departure, I was unable to move. Gradually, I started to regain my normal consciousness while the enchanting form of Mother Kali simultaneously disappeared. My body felt numb, as if it was paralyzed. A few minutes passed before I could move a little, and the protruding tongue also withdrew into my mouth, but I could not yet move my bulging, transfixed eyes. Only after massaging them for a while, I felt them come back to normal. My throat was in severe pain due to the roaring laughter. Looking down, I found that Amma's prasad was still clasped in my hand."

Hearing this narration, Amma simply sat there with a gracious, all-knowing smile playing on her lips.

CHAPTER 3

The Ashram is Born

IN 1982, AMMA'S ASHRAM was officially registered as a non-profit charitable institution. At that time, the ashram consisted of only about ten of us including Amma. When Gayatri and I came to settle in Vallickavu in early 1980, only one *brahmachari* named Unnikrishnan was staying there full time. A devotee of the Divine Mother, he left his home and became a wandering monk. In 1976, he became Amma's first spiritual son and continued leading an austere life, engaged in the daily ritual worship of the Divine Mother in the small temple where Amma held the Devi Bhava three nights a week. In those days, we all stayed in a small thatched hut whenever we got time to rest, which was very rarely. Seeing that some people were allowed to settle permanently near Amma, others also wanted to do the same. It was at this time that Balu, Venu, Sreekumar, Ramakrishnan, Rao and a few others came to stay.

Amma was very discriminating about who could stay in the ashram. She considered many factors: whether their family would suffer financially on account of their child not earning any money for supporting them, how serious they were about their spiritual aspirations, and what was the depth of the relationship of each person with herself. She had a very clear vision of the future and had a definite intention behind every action. Her very birth was for the spiritual good of the world, and to that end, she felt that a group of young people should be trained in spiritual life, disciples whom she could send out to different parts of India and the world to spread real spirituality.

In the last century, there was a great soul, Sri Ramakrishna Paramahamsa of Bengal, who also had a similar mission. He gave all of his energy to the spiritual improvement of the devotees, even at the cost of his health and life, and finally trained a group of young men to carry out his work. There are countless numbers of people who consider him as an Incarnation of the Lord, who intentionally came into this world for a particular purpose, not helplessly thrown into it by the force of past *karma*. Similarly, there are many who feel this about Amma, that she is the Divine Mother Herself, who has come to this world with the very specific purpose of spiritually uplifting the world. The Lord declares in the Bhagavad Gita that He will be born into this world of matter whenever the need arises to protect dharma (righteousness) from the decaying influence of Time:

> Whenever there is a decay of religion, O Bharata, and an ascendancy of irreligion, then I manifest Myself. For the protection of the good, for the destruction of evil-doers, for the firm establishment of religion, I am born in every age.
>
> —Ch.4, v.7-8

Since the very nature of Time is change, the world requires constant spiritual maintenance, so to say. And so, the Supreme must descend again and again.

Once in the days when there were only a few people staying near Amma, she was discussing the purpose of her birth. She told us that she would train a large group of young aspirants to spread spiritual knowledge to mankind. She also said that the day would come when she would have to travel around the world many times in order to give peace to the people outside the holy land of India. Her words shocked and worried everyone. She had never been more than a few miles outside of the village, and if she were to go around the world, who would look after her? And who would look after those staying here with her? We thought that perhaps she was just joking.

Amma with Shakti Prasad

It was at this time that Amma revealed the uniqueness of Shakti Prasad, her *manasa putra* or mind-born son, as she called him. She hinted that he would become a major force for good in the world, being a partial Incarnation of the Divine Amma, brought into existence by Amma's own will! There is a story in the scriptures of India about a sage named Vishwamitra who created a world for his devotee, Trisankhu, to live in. There is also a story in the Vedantic book, *Yoga Vasishtha,* which mentions the creation of a world by a boy sage. On one occasion, when I had asked her if the ancient sages could really create through their will power as mentioned in these stories, she replied, "Certainly. Didn't Amma create Shakti Prasad?" This may sound like a tall claim to those who don't know Shakti's history, but I have no doubt that there has rarely been a child born under such unusual circumstances.

Shakti's parents were Vidyadharan and Omana from a village about five miles from Amma's ashram. They had not been blessed with any children, even after nine years of marriage. Hearing of Amma's miraculous divine powers, they decided to take a chance and ask her to bless them with a child. The two of them arrived at the ashram in 1977, but before Omana could say anything to Amma, she called her and said, "Daughter, I know that you want a child. I will remove your sorrow and you will become pregnant four months from today. Don't worry." Sure enough, after four months, Omana started to show signs of pregnancy. After the fourth month, she went to the hospital for an examination. The doctors confirmed her pregnancy, but what was her surprise when, during the ninth month, the same doctors declared that there was no child in her womb! The mystery was that her belly was still fully distended as in a woman about to deliver. Different tests were done and all showed negative results. At last, an x-ray was taken, and to the astonishment of the doctors, only a dense cloud was found within her womb. She was then taken to different hospitals for consultation, but none of the doctors could come to any conclusion about whether or not there was a child in the womb.

Omana came to the Amma in a dejected mood, but Amma consoled her, "Be courageous; that child is divine and no x-ray will be able to photograph it." Days and months passed. The neighbors poked fun at her, saying that she was going to give birth to an elephant! Yet, Omana and her husband never lost faith in Amma. It was their biggest test. Finally, during the sixteenth month of her pregnancy, Amma told Omana to go to the hospital for delivery. Despite her huge belly, the doctors could not find any signs of a child. After much discussion, they finally

The Ashram is Born

decided on a cesarean. Upon completing the operation, they were astounded to find a healthy male child in her womb. Amma gave him the name "Shakti Prasad," which means "Blessing of the Divine Energy."

Shakti started meditating at the age of three and would sit repeating "Om Namah Shivaya" or "Salutations to the Auspicious One" with his eyes closed. Whenever he came to the ashram, he would go directly to Amma and sit next to her, putting flowers on her feet. Once some of the visitors made fun of him saying, "Hey, what do you think of when you close your eyes?" He retorted, "What do you know? I see a beautiful light made of changing colors in my forehead!" Amma says that when she feels that the right time has come, she will remove the little screen of ignorance which she has kept in his mind so that he will then know himself to be one with God. It is then that his real stature will reveal itself and his work will begin in this world.

After explaining these things, Amma smiled. One of the boys who was sitting nearby said, "Gosh, Amma, you have a pretty good plan." Amma looked at him with an expression of amusement on her face and said, "Thanks, I'm glad you approve!"

A regular visitor to the ashram was one of the villagers named Bhargavan. He would come to the ashram for every Bhava darshan and fully believed that at that particular time the soul of Sri Krishna had entered Amma's body. It was not unusual for a person to think like this, for such beliefs are an integral part of the religious life in villages like Amma's. The simple folk have no idea of what Self-Realization is or what the Vision of God is. Their use for God goes as far as someone who can grant their prayers and fulfill their wishes. Though they feel that God is all-pervading, they consider Him most easily approachable in a temple and that He is pleased with ritual offerings. If He is given the things He likes, then He is inclined to bless His devotees with what they want—such is the simplicity of the villagers' beliefs. The idea that God is within each one's heart as the Inner Reality beyond the individual ego never occurs to them. Therefore, the only way that they could interpret Amma's highly unusual behavior was by thinking that God was temporarily possessing her during the Bhava darshans. Thus, when Bhargavan came for darshan, he really felt that he was seeing Krishna Himself, and he had no conception of Amma's spiritual greatness. He thought that she was just a very lucky village girl who was a recipient of God's grace.

One day, he told Amma that he was going to go to the famous Krishna temple at Guruvayoor, which is about a hundred and fifty miles north of the ashram. Amma said to him, "Are you going to be able to see Krishna there?" "Of course, otherwise, why would I go so far?" he replied. He then left and reached Guruvayoor in the evening, but unfortunately, he had forgotten to take his spectacles, and therefore he could not see the image of the Lord; he could only see a hazy shape. Returning home disappointed, he went for Amma's darshan during Krishna Bhava. Smiling mischievously, Amma said, "Did you forget your eyeglasses? When I am *here*, why did you go *there* to see Me?" Needless to say, Bhargavan lost all interest in visiting temples from then on.

If one wanted to see what Lord Krishna was like, one could do so by seeing Amma in Krishna Bhava. Krishna's name means "the one who attracts" and He was said to be the most charming of all beings. This was also the impression while standing before Amma during the Krishna Bhava. She seemed to be a mixture of omniscience and mischief. She would offer a piece of banana to someone, and when they were about to bite into it, she would suddenly pull it away! This, of course, would send waves of laughter around the room, but one would not be embarrassed, for was it not God Himself who engaged in this play? Sometimes she would pour some sacred water into someone's mouth and keep pouring until it would run down their front onto the floor. If someone had offered her butter, she would hold it out in front of them to take a bite, and when they would try, she would smear it on their nose! Her actions tallied with the stories one reads about the Lord's play during His childhood in Brindavan.

One day, a couple of months after settling down in the ashram, Balu, one of the brahmacharis, and I were in the hut. I was listening with earphones to a recording of Amma singing, when she came in and started singing the exact same tune in time with the tape. She could not possibly have heard anything coming from the earphones, as I had turned the volume down very low. I looked at her with a shocked expression and asked her how she knew what I was listening to. She simply gave a knowing smile and went to the other end of the hut. She seemed to be playing with a towel, trying to tie it around her head. At last she turned around with a turban on her head and shot a glance at us. What was our surprise when we saw her in Krishna Bhava! After a moment, she turned away from us and again turned towards us. She was now her usual self. It was after this incident that we became convinced that Amma's Divine Moods were entirely in her hands, to show or not to show as and when she pleased. Until then, Amma had innocently averred that her Bhavas were in the hands of God. We now came to know her secret: that she and the Lord were one. In an unusual mood, Amma said, "If you want to see the Krishna that lived five thousand years ago in Brindavan, you can see Him here (pointing to herself). The Divine Amma and Lord Krishna both reside within this crazy girl!"

CHAPTER 4

The First Disciples

A FEW MONTHS BEFORE MY meeting Amma at the end of 1979, Balu (now Swami Amritaswarupananda Puri) came to Amma. He was a college student at that time and was particularly talented in music and drama. He had heard that there was someone possessing divine powers in Vallickavu, and so he came one day to see for himself. Devotional by nature from childhood, he was deeply moved by the fervor with which Amma sang songs to God. Amma immediately understood him to be one of her own. When he went for darshan, he could not contain his tears, so overwhelmed was he by Amma's pure, motherly affection. Though he went home after the darshan, he was never again the same. His mind became full of the thought of Amma and the longing to see her possessed him. This pattern was to repeat itself again and again with all of Amma's close devotees.

One night, Balu awoke smelling a divine fragrance in his room. The next moment he felt someone gently stroking his forehead and was shocked to see that it was

Amma. She smiled at him and said, "My son, Amma is always with you. Do not worry." Before he could say a word, she vanished.

Needless to say, Balu could not believe his eyes. The next morning, he rushed to Vallickavu in order to confirm the authenticity of his vision, but he was disappointed to find that Amma was not there. He went without food the whole day while waiting for her. When she finally returned in the evening, she went straight to the kitchen and brought a plate of rice which she fed him with her own hands. Then she said, "Son, last night Amma came to you!" Hearing these words, Balu was overwhelmed by the thought of Amma's affection for him, and broke down crying.

Balu came to stay near Amma around the same time that Gayatri and I settled there. She used to subject him to severe tests to see whether he really wanted to renounce everything and dedicate himself to spiritual life. She sent him out for a job about fifty miles away from the ashram, asking him to stay in the house of a devotee. He was not there for more than a few weeks when he returned to the ashram, refusing to go back to work; he could not bear the separation from Amma. Amma then decided to have him study for an M.A. in philosophy. After much searching, he finally found a professor who would tutor him in the subject, but this man was not inclined to come to the ashram. After much coaxing, he did agree to visit but did not want to see Amma. Leaving him in one place off to the side, Balu went to sing before Amma during the Devi Bhava. What was his surprise when he saw the professor rushing into the temple and prostrating at full length at Amma's feet! Needless to say, the professor regularly came to the ashram from then on to instruct Balu in philosophy and to enjoy the darshan of Amma. In due course, Balu passed his M.A. exams.

Venu (now Swami Pranavamritananda Puri) was Balu's younger brother. When he heard about Amma from his brother, he was not at all inclined to go and see her. He disdainfully said, "I won't go to see that fishergirl." On hearing this, Amma said, "He is also my son and will come here." Amma's words worried Balu, for there was already a commotion in his house over the fact that he had renounced worldly life and had settled in the ashram. What would happen if another of his parents' sons were to do the same?

One day, Amma went for a visit to Balu's aunt's house where Venu was residing during his college studies. Seeing her there, Venu walked past her, ignoring her completely. Not to be put off by his rudeness, Amma went over to him, and holding his hands in her own, she lovingly said,

"Aren't you the brother of my son Balu? Amma has been yearning to see you." Venu's barriers immediately broke down before Amma's innocent motherly love. Looking at each other, some of us whispered, "The deal's closed. He's finished!" and laughed. And sure enough, he was finished. Although Venu somehow managed to complete his studies and pass the examinations, he had lost all interest in worldly life and in a spirit of renunciation, soon shaved his head of its long hair and came to the ashram to stay.

Sreekumar (Swami Purnamritananda Puri) lived in a village about ten miles away from Balu's. He heard about Amma and came to see her in 1979. It was a crucial period of his life as his mind was assailed by doubts regarding the existence of God. "If God exists, how is it that few are happy and the majority suffer in this world?" This thought tormented Sreekumar and he felt that perhaps he could find the answer from Amma. Upon seeing her and her loving glance, and feeling the divine presence and holy atmosphere that pervaded everything around her, his mind was full of bliss. Yet he was baffled by Amma's highly unusual behavior. At times she behaved like a small and innocent child and played with the devotees. Sometimes she would sing and dance, and at other times she wept in the ecstasy of longing for God. One moment she would be deeply absorbed in meditation, and the next moment she would be rolling on the ground with laughter. Amma fed Sreekumar with her own hands and instructed him in spiritual principles soon after his arrival. Her holiness, motherly love and unusual, ecstatic behavior bound him to her, and it was not long before Sreekumar decided to settle near Amma. Yet this was not to be for some time, for his parents were not inclined to let him go. He was their only son and was expected to care for them after their retirement. Therefore, after graduating from college, he was sent off to work in a distant place.

Sreekumar's fate was the same as Balu's; he simply could not stay away from Amma and hold a job. He led a miserable existence in Bangalore, absentmindedly doing his work while thinking of Amma. After one month, he returned home with a high fever and was immediately hospitalized. Lying in the hospital, he had the following experience:

"My father had gone out to get some coffee for me. I was alone in the room when all of a sudden my hands and legs became as if paralyzed. A cool and gentle breeze blew over me, and to my great surprise, I saw Amma entering the room. With a benign smile on her face, she walked towards me. Like a small child, I started crying. She then sat near me and put my head on her lap without speaking a word. I was overcome with emotion, words getting stuck in my throat. An effulgence from Amma's body pervaded the room and she herself was surrounded by a divine light. Just then, the door opened and my father walked in. At that point, Amma immediately vanished." Sreekumar eventually became a permanent resident of the ashram.

Ramesh Rao (Swami Amritatmananda Puri) was the favorite son of a wealthy cloth merchant and was working in his father's shop. But the slow-paced life of his village did not appeal to him. He wished to go abroad to the Persian Gulf for work and was in the process of trying to secure a job there when he heard about Amma's divine powers. It was in June of 1979 that he came to Vallickavu for the first time, seeking to know about his future. Little did he suspect what great changes were in store for him. Before he could say anything to Amma, she told him, "Son, you are trying to go across the ocean. Amma will make it possible if you wish. Do not worry."

Those knowing words were the beginning of the end of Rao's worldly life and the start of his spiritual one. He went home and tried to attend to his business in the cloth shop, but found it impossible to concentrate his mind in that direction; he only longed to see Amma again. This longing became so intense that he would close the shop early on many days and rush to Vallickavu. He started to have many dreams of the Goddess of the Universe who appeared to him in Amma's form. Day by day his restlessness increased along with his desire to realize God. And where is the wonder in that? In Amma's presence, one finds that the mind naturally goes towards God and godly thoughts.

One day, while sitting next to Amma, Rao lost all consciousness of the world, and for more than five hours, he experienced that he was a two year old child floating on the Ocean of the Blissful Divine Mother. Amma finally called him and brought him back to this world of name and form. After this experience, Rao lost what little taste was left in him for the pleasures of the world. He stopped going to his shop and spent weeks on end with Amma and the other resident devotees. This naturally caused much agitation in his family. Though nearly everyone in India knows that God-Realization is the real goal of life, parents very rarely wish that their children become renunciates, dedicating their lives to that sublime goal. They feel that one should enjoy the pleasures of married life, accumulate wealth and property and then, in old age, practice spiritual sadhana. They forget, however, that by the time one reaches old age (if one does not die before that!), one's mind is so set in its ways that it is all but impossible to concentrate on God. How can one concentrate on God after dwelling on worldly objects for seventy or eighty years? Can an old dog learn new tricks? Many years ago in India, it was compulsory for children to be sent away from home at a very young age and be lodged in a *gurukulam* (the house or ashram of a traditional teacher). There one would study and chant the ancient scriptures, selflessly serve one's elders and teacher, practice control of the senses and lead a simple and noble life. Only after twelve years of that kind of disciplined life would one get married if one wished and enjoy material wealth and worldly pleasure. But even then, one was not to give up scriptural studies, worship, and a modicum of self-control. After begetting virtuous children, one was supposed to leave family life by the age of fifty and either live in an ashram or a forest, dedicating the rest of one's life to concentrated spiritual practice with the goal of realizing God. If one had cultivated a strong foundation in one's youth and continued on into middle age, it was not with much difficulty that a transition could be made to a life of total renunciation and self-control. That was the ideal in the old days. Nowadays no one follows such a course of life-long training. To lead a totally worldly life for seventy years, do a little prayer, worship and go to the temple every once in a while, and then expect that one will be able to concentrate on God at the end and finally merge in Him, is very wishful thinking. If that were enough to attain Self-Realization, then why have so many people strained themselves to their utmost by struggling their whole lives to control the wandering mind and fix it on the Supreme?

The present day world being what it is, there is no wonder that Rao's parents were not inclined to let him become a monk, for it was obvious that he was heading in that direction at full speed. Amma told Rao to go home and get the permission of his parents to stay in the ashram. That was like asking a juicy mouse to beg leave of two husky and hungry cats! "Amma, they will make trouble for me if I go there now," Rao protested. "A courageous man is one who can overcome all difficulties," Amma calmly replied. She was not going to accept Rao in monastic life so easily. He had been strongly inclined towards a worldly life before coming to her and she wanted to make sure that he had the inner stuff, the makings of a monk, before letting him renounce the world forever. How seemingly cruel and wise she is!

After going home, Rao's parents retained him there by force. Seeing no change in his attitude, they decided that his sudden other-worldliness might be due to some form of mental disease. After ten days of treatment in a mental hospital, his parents then took him to some other relatives far away from his own village where they tried to tempt him through tricks, using a young female relative as the bait, but he withstood all temptations. Rao wrote to Amma, "If Amma doesn't save me, I will commit suicide!" After one month, he was allowed to return to his village as it seemed that his "craziness" had gone. How unfortunate it is, yet not surprising, that people of the world think that the love of God and the desire to directly experience Him are abnormal. The gems of mankind have been those people who manifested some devotion to God in their daily lives. Abraham Lincoln, Albert Einstein, Mahatma Gandhi—all are looked upon by the worldly-minded as great men. Yet these men attributed their little bit of greatness to God; they were all humble devotees of the Lord. Why then do people of the world think that whole-hearted devotion to God is an aberration of the mind? Doesn't the Old Testament say to love the Lord with all one's heart, with all one's soul and with all one's mind? Who is crazy, the one who loves God or the one who doesn't even think of Him? Such is the power of Maya, the Universal Illusion, that makes people see everything topsy-turvy.

After returning to his village, Rao once again came to the ashram. Amma insisted that he return home until his parents gave permission of their own free will for him to stay near her. This was unacceptable to Rao, so he would not go. Within a few days, his father, relatives and a van load of police showed up at the ashram. As they tried to take him away with them, Rao declared, "I am old enough to decide where and how I will live my life." The police, however, did not care for his words and forced him into a car in order to take him once again to a mental hospital.

Had Amma abandoned her helpless son? Not by any means! On the way to the hospital, everyone got out to eat at a restaurant. Rao refused to join them and sat in the car. Just then he heard a voice within him saying, "If you escape now, you will be saved. Otherwise, you will be destroyed!" The next moment, he saw a vehicle for hire which had stopped in front of his car. Without wasting a moment, he jumped into it and asked the driver to take him to the house of a devotee who lived in the same town. From there, he left by a night train to Bombay and when finally discovered there, proceeded further north to the Himalayas. Wandering as a penniless beggar without even warm clothing, he stayed in the Himalayan region for many months. At last, Amma wrote a letter telling him that the danger was over and that he should come to the ashram. With money sent by the ashramites, Rao returned and settled down as a resident of the ashram in 1982, only after having his mettle severely tried by Amma. Now she could be sure that he would stick to his resolve till the end. Such should be the resoluteness of one's determination to go beyond all obstacles and realize the indwelling Truth, God.

Ramakrishnan (Swami Ramakrishnananda Puri) started to visit Amma in 1978. He was an employee of a bank located near her village. From the beginning, Amma's loving nature melted his heart and bound him to her. His chosen aspect of God was the Divine Mother Meenakshi as embodied in the form of the Goddess installed in the famous Madurai Meenakshi Temple in Tamil Nadu. Due to his intense longing to behold Her, Amma's grace was invoked and she blessed Ramakrishnan with many visions of the Goddess. What is not possible to achieve even after years of strenuous effort is easily gained by the grace of a Realized Soul.

Amma tested Ramakrishnan's faith many times both before and after his coming to stay in the ashram in 1984. Though the Guru is always aware of his or her own omnipresence and omnipotence, the disciple is not. It is the Guru's duty to instill that faith in the disciple so that sadhana will be pursued with intense zeal and certainty. Ramakrishnan had been entrusted with the duty of opening the vault every morning in the bank where he worked, and so he was expected to be at the bank by ten o'clock sharp. His job was located about sixty-five miles from Amma's village. After the Sunday night darshan at the ashram, Ramakrishnan boarded a bus on Monday and left for work. The bus, however, stopped at a place about eight miles before his destination. He then got out and inquired about the next bus, but became worried upon hearing that it would not be able to get him to his office before ten o'clock. He then tried to get a taxi but to no avail. Understandably upset, he cried out to Amma, "O Amma!" hoping that she would find some way out for him. After all, he had gone to the ashram on Sunday out of devotion to her, in order to serve her at that time during Devi Bhava. Was it not her duty to look after him? Within a few moments, a stranger drove up on a motor scooter and offered him a ride to the town where he was headed. Reaching there, he walked into the bank at exactly ten! When he related this miracle to Amma, she commented, "One call is enough if done with concentration. God will come."

One day, Amma said to Ramakrishnan in a serious tone, "There are some men who still look at girls even after taking up a life of renunciation." Ramakrishnan asked her, "Who is that, Amma?" "You!" she replied.

The First Disciples

"Who, me? Amma is finding fault with me, though I am innocent," he objected.

"Isn't there a woman working at the desk next to yours who wears a nose ring and don't you look at her every day? But don't worry, son. I know that you look at her because she reminds you of me," Amma replied with a laugh.

After Ramakrishnan had left for work, Amma told me about the incident and said with a giggle, "Ramakrishnan got a glimpse of Amma's siddhis (mystic powers) today!"

These were some of Amma's disciples who were destined to become sannyasis or renunciates. I use the word "destined" because such people do not procrastinate or calculate before leaving worldly life for a life of renunciation. They simply do not see any other alternative. They cannot bear and will not accept any other life style. This should not lead one to believe that married people or those who are not monks cannot achieve true spirituality. I once heard Amma say the following to a group of married devotees:

"A householder can certainly attain Realization, but he or she must be a real householder (*grahasthashrami*). Though he lives with his family, he should live the life of an ashramite, living only for God. That is real *grahasthashrama* or married life. It is possible to carry on a spiritual life while living in the world. The one condition is that one should perform one's actions selflessly, without any attachment, surrendering everything at the feet of the Lord. All one's actions should be performed with absolute dedication. The householder should constantly use his discrimination thinking, 'Everything is God's; nothing is mine. God alone is my true Father, Mother, Relative and Friend.'

"A householder who wishes to lead a spiritual life after completing his responsibilities in the world, should exercise renunciation from the very beginning, because it won't come easily. Renunciation demands constant and long-term practice. He may not be able to relinquish everything externally, but he should try to be detached within. In order to keep this spirit of inner detachment, *lakshya bodha* (a spiritually goal-oriented mind) is important.

"A good householder should be a sannyasi internally. Amma does not say that a person should run away from his duties. He should perform his duties to the best of his ability. It is not good to run away from life; that is cowardice. A person who runs away from life is not fit to be a spiritual seeker. That is why Krishna did not let Arjuna run away from the battlefield. Life is a battle. It is not something to be avoided. Furthermore, you cannot

The First Disciples

avoid it. You may run to a remote forest or to an ashram to escape from life, but life will follow you there as well. Just as you cannot run away from death, you cannot run away from life; you can only try to transcend both. Therefore, an intelligent person does not try to escape life, but lives it sensibly, giving proper attention to his affairs.

"The wise way of life is to have a good spiritual foundation. As far as possible, try to be detached as much as possible, so that you can prepare yourself for total renunciation. But since most people are not sannyasis, they should play their part well in the world.

"To show compassion towards suffering humanity is our obligation to God. Our spiritual quest should begin with selfless service to the world. People will be disappointed if they sit in meditation, expecting a third eye to open after closing the other two. This is not going to happen. We cannot close our eyes to the world in the name of spirituality and expect to evolve. To behold unity while viewing the world through open eyes is spiritual Realization.

"Whether one is a householder or a sannyasi, renunciation is the means to the end. Internally, a householder should be a sannyasi. Externally he should be active, performing his duties neatly and well. As a person who leads a spiritual life while leading a family life, prepare yourself for the final letting go.

"A sannyasi is one who has dedicated his entire life, both external and internal, for others, for the good of the world. A grahasthasrami is one who still leads a family life externally, but a sannyasi's life internally.

"A householder may not be able to renounce things so easily, but he should try to quieten his mind. A householder's mind tends to be noisy with all the problems that disturb him from every direction. Amma knows that it is very difficult to overcome these problems which make thunderous noises in your head. But it is not impossible to obtain inner silence. Most of our ancient masters were householders. They could do it. They were also human beings. So if they had the power to do it, we can do it.

"The potential of being a true renunciate exists in everyone. It may be in seed form, but it is there. The seedling will not germinate by itself; you need to sow it, fence it in to guard it from stray animals, protect it from too much sun and rain, give it enough water, and thus care for it well. It will then grow into a huge, shade-giving tree, yielding an abundance of fruits and flowers. This kind of effort is needed to attain the goal. The saints and sages did *tapas* (austerities), and thus attained the goal.

The First Disciples

We should also try to attain the goal with steadfastness.

"Sri Krishna was a householder. He had many responsibilities, but he was the embodiment of detachment. Sri Rama was also a householder, and in addition to that, a king. He was the embodiment of dharma. King Janaka was a king and a householder. He, too, was a *Jivanmukta*, a Liberated soul. They all found enough time to do tapas and to lead a spiritual life, even in the midst of all their court duties and other problems. If we say that we have no time because of our problems and family responsibilities, that is no excuse; it simply means that we have no real desire to follow the path of spirituality.

"A grahasthashrami should be able to renounce everything whenever he wants. He should be like a bird sitting on a dry twig. The bird knows that the twig will break at any moment; and therefore, it is ready to take off at any time. Likewise, a householder should always have the awareness that worldly relationships are momentary and may end at any time. Like the bird, he should be ready to cast off all bonds and leap into spirituality. He should have the firm faith that all the actions he is involved in are just temporary works entrusted to him by God. Like a faithful servant, he should be able to do everything without any sense of ownership. Whenever God, the Master, asks him to stop, he should be able to do so. He knows that nothing is his. A householder should be ready to give up all pleasures and worldly comforts whenever he wants to do so. He should do his duty in the world, but as a sadhana, as a form of worship.

"Stay at home, but stay in touch with your true Self, the real Center of existence. Follow the instructions of a true Master. Recognize the prison you are in for what it is, and understand that it is not your real home, and that your attachments are not ornaments but chains of bondage. A true Master will help you realize this. Once that realization takes place, it doesn't matter whether you are at home or in an ashram. No matter what you do or where you are, you cannot move from your real Center."

CHAPTER 5

Amma as the Guru

AT THE TIME THAT MOST OF US came to settle at Amma's feet, her attitude was either that of a child or a mother. At times she would act like a youngster, running about, dancing and playing with the other children. She would rest under the trees, eat off the ground and would lie outside in the rain. Like a doting mother, she was very affectionate towards everyone and did not insist upon any discipline. She would feed us with her own hands, make sure we had something on which to sleep, comfort us in our sicknesses and other difficulties, and kept an eye on us all the time. But after some time, she declared that soon she would change her role and start to treat us as a Guru would his disciples. This was fine with me. I had been longing for an ashram atmosphere to come up around Amma. And sure enough, the childlike aspect of Amma practically disappeared; her motherly nature receded into the background and she became the Teacher.

Amma could identify with any role that she decided to take on. During the Krishna and Devi Bhavas, she was the embodiment of those aspects of God. When she was in the mood of a child, she was just like a child. She could be more motherly than one's own mother. Now Amma became a Guru of gurus. Where is the wonder in this? It is by the Grace of the Universal Mother that all the great Gurus became who they were. When the Goddess decides to live in that role, it is child's play for Her.

During the end of November 1982, Amma and a group of us went to Tiruvannamalai for a ten-day pilgrimage. This was the first time that Amma was leaving the village for such a long time, and also the first time that the Krishna and Devi Bhavas would not be held since their inception in 1975. We took a train on a Monday morning after the Sunday night darshan and arrived the next day. There were about forty or fifty of us, and we all stayed in the two houses that I had built while I had been residing there. Amma gave darshan in the house in the daytime. Many devotees who were living in and around Ramanashram came. In the evenings she sang devotional songs in the ashram in front of Ramana Maharshi's tomb or *samadhi* shrine as it is called. The next morning, a sannyasi named Kunju Swami came to visit Amma. He

Arunachala Hill and Temple in Tiruvannamalai

had been born in Kerala and was a disciple of the famous saint Narayana Guru, who had lived at the beginning of the century. Narayana Guru had brought him to Tiruvannamalai when he was a young man and entrusted him to Ramana Maharshi for his spiritual upbringing. Now he was already in his eighties, but Amma treated him like a five year old boy and he enjoyed it like a child would with his own mother. When he sat in meditation, she would place her hand on his shaved head and dance a little "ditty" while going round and round him. A friend of mine in Tiruvannamalai told me that when I left to stay with Amma in the beginning of 1980, Kunju Swami had said, "Nealu would have never left this place until his death if the Amma there in Kerala were anyone but *Parashakti* (the Supreme Energy)." And you could see in his expression that he indeed looked upon Amma as the Goddess Incarnate.

One day, Amma suddenly bolted out of our residence all alone. This was obviously an escape; she clearly did not want anyone to follow her. Since I was the only person who saw her leave, I immediately grabbed some bananas, cookies, and drinking water, put them in a bag and ran after her. Having witnessed Amma's lack of body-consciousness, I knew that she might very well get lost. I followed her from a distance as she walked around Arunachala Hill, obviously in an intoxicated mood. Seeing me running out of the house, all the others followed on my heels. Soon they all overtook me and joined Amma, who by this time was walking at a very rapid pace. Gradually she disappeared into the distance and I was left behind.

Talking to Sreekumar afterwards, I got the following report of what happened. He said, "A person came running to us and said, 'Amma is missing. She is nowhere to be found!' Hearing this, we immediately hired a horse-cart and started driving towards Arunachala Hill, looking intently for Amma. The previous day, while climbing the hill with her, we had come across many caves on both sides. Amma would go into some of them to meditate and it was often only after much urging that she could be persuaded to come out. While descending from the mountain, Amma had said, "I don't feel like coming down, but thinking of you children, I am restraining myself." So we guessed that Amma might be sitting in one of those caves, but how to find Amma among the numberless caves on this vast hill? Everyone was worried.

"The horse-cart finally reached the hill. After traveling a few miles, we suddenly caught a glimpse of Amma's form, walking far ahead of us on the road. When we had driven up fairly close to her, we got down off the cart. It was a glorious sight to see Amma. She was swaying to and fro while walking, as if drunk. Her whole body was vibrating, and her hands showed a sacred *mudra* (mystic hand pose). Her eyes were half-closed, and a blissful smile glowed on her face. It looked as if the Goddess Parvati was circumambulating Lord Shiva! We followed her and instructed the horse-cart also to follow us. We began chanting Vedic mantras and loudly singing bhajans. The hills echoed with our chanting. The bliss of samadhi that radiated from Amma, together with the joy of singing and chanting, blessed all of us with a sublime experience.

"After we had followed Amma for some distance, she turned around and cast a glance of indescribable love on us. Her gaze held so much compassion and power that it seemed she was burning away all our karmas and *vasanas* (deep-rooted habits)! Slowly Amma came down to our level. Soon she was laughing and talking with us affectionately. A little tired by the long walk, she sat down under a tree at the roadside for a few minutes. Despite our suggestions, she refused to get into the horse-cart, and was soon up and walking again. Thus, we all walked for the full eight miles around the hill.

"Towards the end of the circumambulation, we saw a snake charmer playing his flute by the side of the road. Amma went and sat before him, watching with great interest as the snake danced to the music of the flute. Like a little child, Amma asked, 'Children, why don't snakes have hands and feet?' Her innocent question made us all laugh. She herself then gave the answer: 'In their previous births, they might not have used their hands and legs properly. Children, keep in mind that such a birth could come to anyone who misuses what God has given him.'

"Now her facial expression had completely changed, revealing the seriousness and majesty of the Guru. 'Children,' she continued, 'Amma knows that you love Amma more than anything else. You cannot think of any form of God other than Amma. Therefore, you do not really have to circumambulate the hill. However, you must become a role model for society and should set an example for them to follow. In olden days, people were able to see God in their gurus. But, in the present age, not many people have that power of discernment. Therefore, such conventional rites and rituals are required for an ordinary man. From your own example society has to learn to follow these practices. So, in the future, always honor such rituals in order to uplift mankind. Amma herself does these practices to teach you the proper path.'

"We all sat in chastened silence, absorbing Amma's words. After a few moments, Amma continued, 'Children, don't be sad thinking that Amma is always correcting you. Never think that Amma has no love for you. It is only out of Amma's overflowing love for you that she is instructing you. Children, you are Amma's treasure. When Amma renounced everything, there was only one thing that could not be renounced—that was you, my children. It is only when Amma sees you becoming the Light of the world that Amma truly feels happy. Amma does not require your praise or service. Amma only wants to see you acquire the strength to bear the burdens and sufferings of the world.'

"Amma's profound yet nectar-like words brought our egos crumbling to the ground. Falling at Amma's feet we prayed, 'O Amma, please make us noble! Please make us so pure that our lives may be sacrificed for the salvation of the whole world.'"

After four hours, I at last returned with an empty bag, having eaten all the provisions myself. As I entered the house with the empty bag in my hand, Amma immediately grasped the situation and bursting into laughter, said, "Have you brought something for me to eat?"

Our visit coincided with the Deepam Festival, an annual celebration attended by hundreds of thousands of people from all over southern India. A sacred fire is lit on top of Arunachala Hill representing the light of spiritual illumination blazing forth in the darkness of ageless ignorance. We all went to the town one morning to see the chariot festival. Images of the local deities were placed in a huge, ornately carved wooden chariot more than a hundred feet tall, and a procession was made through the streets with people pulling the chariot by a thick rope. It was a joyous occasion and a sight to behold. While Amma was standing on the balcony of one of the buildings to get a good view of the chariot, an avadhuta named Ramsuratkumar came to see her. He had been a disciple of the well-known Swami Ramdas of Kanhangad in northern Kerala. He was highly revered in Tiruvannamalai for his saintliness. Dressed in rags, he had a long, flowing beard and in his hand he carried a fan. In Amma's presence, he became like a little child, and looked upon her as his spiritual mother. This opened the eyes of the local devotees as to who Amma really was. It was after a blissful ten days in Tiruvannamalai that we all returned to the ashram.

One day Amma decided that it was time to build two huts in addition to the one that we already had. With the influx of permanent residents, some more rooms were needed. Amma did not want us to live out in the open forever. To live so simply was no doubt a good test of our detachment, but Amma thought that a spiritual aspirant should have a space of his own for his sadhana. I was in charge of supervising the work. Some workers had arrived to build the huts. I designed a plan and showed it to Amma. It consisted of three huts facing away from each other in a U-shape. I thought that this would conserve space and make it possible for the breeze to enter through the doorways of each of the huts. It seemed like a good idea. The workers erected the main poles to support the frame and started to tie the coconut leaves on to the frame. Amma came out of the temple and saw what was going on.

"Who told them to do this?" shouted Amma. Everyone pointed at me. Suddenly, I lost my architectural pride. "Who asked you to place the huts in this orientation?" Amma asked me.

"Why Amma, you saw the plan and approved of it," I replied.

"I don't remember seeing any plan. Tear this down! Nobody should build huts facing each other. All you think of is how to be comfortable, how to get a good breeze! Don't you care about scriptural rules? No! The rules do not allow huts to be built like this." Declaring this, Amma went back into the temple. I helplessly turned towards the workers and asked them to tear down the work that they had been doing since morning. I turned to Balu and said,

"What sense is there in this? It is very difficult to understand Amma."

"Wait, be patient. Let us see what Amma has up her sleeve. This is her way of bringing about your surrender," said Balu.

After two minutes, Amma again emerged from the temple. She looked at the workers who were starting to dismantle the huts. "What are they doing? Tell them to build them the way they originally planned. Otherwise, how is the breeze going to enter the huts?" said Amma.

"But Amma, what about the scriptural rules?" I asked.

"Rules? There are no rules for building huts. That's only for regular buildings." After this exclamation, Amma went back into the temple once again.

If bystanders had observed the whole drama that had just taken place, they would have labeled Amma as unreasonable at best, crazy at the worst. But Amma's way of dealing with Her disciples' minds is perfectly in line with the traditions past and present. Marpa, the Guru of the famous Tibetan yogi Milarepa, made his disciple single-handedly build and re-build a seven-story tower before he finally approved of Milarepa's work and granted him initiation. Today Milarepa shines as the greatest yogi of Tibetan history.

There are many such stories about Gurus who have put their disciples through tests of surrender and obedience. One Guru was more than a hundred years old and wanted to appoint a successor. As there were many candidates, he decided to put them all through a test. He asked each one of them to get some earth and to build a mud platform. Everyone ran and got a basket of earth with which they built a platform. When each one was completed, the Guru said, "I am sorry, but these platforms are not as good as I expected them to be. Will you please tear them down and build them over again?"

This was done and then the Guru said, "This is not a suitable place for these. Please tear them down and build them on that piece of land over there."

When this was done, the Guru came to inspect them. "Hmm, I don't like this piece of land either. So why don't you build your platforms over there?"

Many of the disciples thought that the Guru had become senile in his old age and was no longer in full possession of his senses. So, many of them abandoned their work, leaving only a few as candidates to succeed the Guru. But even when these few built up their platforms, the Guru continued to reject them again and again.

After some time, there was only one candidate left, a middle-aged man. Seeing him continue to build and tear down platforms, the other disciples taunted and jeered at him, saying how foolish he was to try to please a Guru who was not in his right mind. This disciple stopped his work for a moment and said to them,

"Brothers, it is not that the *Satguru* (Self-Realized Master) is mad. The whole world is insane, and there is only one who is sane; it is the Satguru. The whole world is blind; only the Satguru can see." They retorted by saying that both he and the Guru were undoubtedly out of their minds. "You may say whatever you like about my humble self, but do not utter a single disrespectful word about my Satguru. Even if I should have to make platforms for the rest of my life in obedience to his wishes, by his grace I will continue to do so," he said.

In the end, the disciple cheerfully made and remade his platform seventy times in all. Then the Guru said to him, "You may stop building now. I am very pleased with you, for you alone have given me implicit obedience and complete surrender to my will and wishes." Turning to the others, he said, "There was not one of you who obeyed me, though this is one of the first rules of being a true disciple—to give the Guru your full love and devotion, to have utter faith in him and obey his wishes with a cheerful heart." The Guru then made the disciple the next Guru of his tradition.

Surrender to a Realized soul is something that happens because of the great love and respect that a disciple feels for him. Putting the disciple through more and more difficult situations only serves to strengthen the disciple's intensity.

As we sat around Amma later that evening, as if intuiting what were my thoughts of the days activities and her strange ways, she said, "Surrender isn't something that can be forced by the Master. Surrender happens naturally within the disciple. There is a change in his attitude, in his understanding, and in the way he does things. A change takes place in the inner world; the whole focus of life changes. A true Master, however, will never force the disciple to surrender. To force in any way would be harmful, like the injury done to a flower bud if you were to forcefully open its petals. Such force would destroy the flower. Opening up is something that happens spontaneously, provided the conducive circumstances are created. The Master creates the necessary situations for this opening up to happen. In reality, a true Master is not a person; he is not the body for he has no ego. His body is just an instrument that he carries around, so that he can be in this world for the benefit of the people. Two persons can force ideas on each other, because they are identified with their egos. But a Satguru, who is an embodiment of the Supreme Consciousness, cannot force anything on anyone, because he is beyond body-consciousness and the mind. The Master is like open space or the boundless sky. He simply exists.

"If someone tries to force their rules or ideas on you, you should know that he is a false teacher, even if he claims to be a Self-Realized Master. A true Master makes no claims about anything. He is simply there. He doesn't care whether you surrender to him or not. If you surrender, you will be benefited; if you don't surrender, you will remain the same. In either case, the Master is untouched. He doesn't worry about anything. In the mere presence of a Master, opening up just happens naturally. The Master doesn't do anything in particular for this to happen. He is the only one who can train you without teaching you directly. His very presence automatically creates a constant wave of situations, wherein you are able to experience the Supreme Reality in all its fullness. But there is no force involved, nor does he make any claims. Surrender will develop within you from the tremendous inspiration you receive through the Master's physical presence, for the Master is the embodiment of all divine qualities. In the Master, you observe true surrender and acceptance, and thus you are given a real example that you can relate to."

This should answer any questions that might have sprung up in the reader's mind. Why does a real Guru sometimes act in an unreasonable, contradictory or even crazy way? It is only to give the disciples the chance to surrender their minds and thereby receive Divine Knowledge. As long as the individual mind exists, the disciple cannot attain Wisdom. The disciple who wants to maintain his or her individuality cannot at the same time merge into the Universal Mind. Surrender and obedience are necessary. Meditation, study and other spiritual disciplines are easy when compared to the practice of surrender to the Guru. Please remember that this is not one person surrendering to another. Any Guru who truly deserves the title has attained unity with the Transcendent Reality. He has merged his individuality in the Universal Existence and has become an instrument of That. Surrendering to him amounts to surrendering to God, merging in God and becoming one with Him. Amma's strange actions and words must be seen in this light.

One day Amma was sitting on the verandah of the temple with her back to the wall. A devotee had brought her a small bag of "mixture," a combination of roasted peanuts, lentils, peas and other dried legumes spiced with salt and chilies. Amma spread it out before her on the cement floor, as was her habit, then picked up a few pieces and ate them. Just then, a group of crows came over and started to peck at the food. One of them started fighting with the rest, trying to prevent them from eating any of the mixture. He finally succeeded in chasing away his brothers and then sat there calmly looking at Amma without eating anything himself. Amma stared at the crow which had an unusually gentle face.

"For some reason I am feeling very affectionate towards that crow. Please give him something to eat," Amma said to me. I went over to give him some mixture, but he jumped away from me and onto Amma's lap. He then sat there for quite a while to the amusement of everyone. Finally, he jumped up again, pecked at Amma's nose ring and flew away.

The next day I was lying down on a mat by the side of the backwaters. The same crow came over to me and jumped onto my belly. He just sat there as long as I kept still. I petted him on the head to which he didn't object. This was all very unusual behavior for a crow, for they are generally very fearful of people or extremely aggressive and arrogant. This crow continued to come for the next few days.

Then one day we found him floating in the water of the uncovered holding tank which was located on top of Amma's room. We brought him down and lit a fire in order to give him some warmth, as he was still alive. Seeing us light a fire by the waterside, Amma came over to find out what was happening. Coming near us, she picked up the dying crow and stroked it gently, whereupon it died in her hands! Blessed crow. Would that we should die like that in the hands of the Divine Mother.

About this time, my mother wrote to me from the United States that she would like to spend some time with me. Once in three or four years she would come either to India or ask me to meet her somewhere midway. This time she wanted to go to Egypt and Israel. With Amma's permission, I left for Bombay, got my visas and plane tickets, and departed for Egypt.

I had never been to the Middle East. Compared to the calm atmosphere of southern India, the feeling there was very hostile. Together we visited the pyramids around Cairo and then went south to the Valley of the Kings and Queens near Karnak. Somehow, a dead culture did not hold much attraction for me. After all, the ancient culture of India is at least as old as the Egyptian civilization was, but the ancient culture of India still survives today as it was thousands of years ago. The only thing that I found really interesting was a very large temple complex in Karnak which had been unearthed by archaeologists in the nineteenth century. It was constructed along the exact same lines as the ancient Shiva temples of Tamil Nadu in India. Similar to Shiva temples, it had large towers which served as gates, and inside were compound walls and pillared halls. There were even images of a god and a goddess, a large tank or pond of water for purificatory bathing and vehicles for taking the god to different places during the year. This was exactly like home! But the scale of the Egyptian temples dwarfed those of India. One felt like a microbe while standing in the great hall of colossal pillars. Thinking that everyone would enjoy seeing these old temples, I bought some slides to take back with me to India.

We then went to Israel. I looked forward to visiting the important places associated with the life of Jesus Christ. After living in India for fifteen years with numerous God-Realized saints, I had developed a real appreciation for Christ as a Realized soul and an Incarnation of God. I thoroughly enjoyed visiting his birth place, the places where some of his miracles were performed, and Calvary, where he breathed his last. I particularly spent more time there meditating. Even though it has been nearly two thousand years since his passing, one can still feel the sanctity of the places that he frequented.

At last I returned to India, glad to be home. The night of my arrival, we decided to show the slides that I had brought from Egypt and Israel. Amma joined us in the meditation hall and I gave a commentary. Amma did not seem very interested until we came to the Egyptian temple that had been dug out of the sand. Seeing that, she said, "See, I have been saying all along that under this meditation hall is my previous ashram. If one were to go deep enough, one would find a temple here along with the tombs of many monks. Everything had been washed over by a tidal wave and got buried in the sand. If archaeologists have found an entire temple complex hundreds of feet beneath the sand in Egypt, why is it not possible that what I am saying is true?"

Amma had occasionally mentioned to us that her previous ashram was under the present one. She also said that there had not been an ashram in this area for at least a thousand years. We therefore put the two statements together and believe that Amma's previous birth must have been at that time. It is probably no accident that of all of Amma's brothers and sisters, it is only she who was actually born in her parents' house. The others were born in hospitals in nearby towns. It is also a well-known fact that a wandering monk had stopped in front of the family house many years ago, when Amma's father was just a young boy, and started to laugh uproariously. When asked why he was laughing, he replied that this was a holy place, that many saints were buried here. One thing is for certain; those who come here can feel an unusual peace pervading the atmosphere. Whether it is due to the holy presence of Amma or the associations of the past, or both, who can say?

Amma says that a place becomes holy not by itself but due to the fact that a saint or sage has lived there. The effect of their radiant aura remains there even after thousands of years. There are many unseen principles that affect our world. Living in Amma's company, one naturally develops faith in these subtle truths.

Seeing the slides of Christian holy places, a lively discussion ensued concerning the vast differences between the original principles of love and renunciation taught by Jesus and the later forms of Christianity that evolved, sometimes resulting in wars and strife. Amma got to the core of the problem immediately by telling us, "The essential principles of all religions teach love, peace, and harmony. The spiritual Masters have never preached selfishness, nor have they ever encouraged people to treat each other unjustly or to fight each other. The problem does not lie in religion or spirituality; it lies within the human mind. The conflicts and problems that exist today, in the name of religion, are due to the lack of proper understanding about religious principles.

"In this modern age, people live more from their minds than from their hearts. The mind is confused and confusing. The mind is the dwelling place of selfishness and unrighteousness. The mind is the seat of all our doubts, and the intellect is the seat of the ego. When you dwell entirely in the mind and ego, you are not concerned about others; you are thinking only about yourself.

"Intellectuals interpret the teachings of the scriptures and the Masters of their religions to suit their own ideas. Unsuspecting people fall easy prey to those distorted definitions of the truth, and end up in conflict with themselves and others. This is what happens in modern society. The intellectuals become leaders and revered advisors. Their followers idealize them and worship them as God. In fact, God has been forgotten; the truth and the essential principles of religion, the very purpose of religion and religious practices, are being ignored.

"Unfortunately, after the death of the Master, most religions are led by such intellectuals. Only a soul filled with love and compassion can guide humanity and throw light on the path of religion. Such a Master alone can unite people and help them to understand the true import of religion and religious principles. But the heart has been forgotten.

"No one who has any real understanding of religion can blame religion and the true religious Masters for the present day calamities which are taking place in the name of religion. It is the fault of the pseudo religious teachers and not their innocent followers. The so-called teachers want to force their own ideas and visions on others. Their innocent followers have full faith in their words, in their false interpretations. The intellect (the ego) is much more powerful than the mind. The mind is intrinsically weak. The intellect has determination, whereas the mind is always doubting, vacillating, and unsteady. The intellectual interpreters of almost all religions have the determination to convince people. Their enormous egos and their determination can easily overpower the followers of any true religion and thus they win their victory over innocent believers.

"Such intellectuals are completely lacking in real faith, love, or compassion. Their mantra is money, power, and prestige. Therefore, do not blame religion, spirituality, or the true Masters for the problems in the world today. There is nothing wrong with spirituality or true religion. The problem lies in the human mind."

When I first settled down near Amma in January of 1980, the only buildings were her family's house, the small *kalari* or temple where she gave darshan during Krishna and Devi Bhavas, and a thatched shelter without any walls in which visiting devotees could rest out of the rain or sun. For some time, I used to sleep in the house, and Amma and Gayatri would rest in the temple. Cooking was done by her family. But after a while, we wanted to be separate from the family, for they could never have the same attitude as we had towards Amma. They always looked upon her as their daughter or sister. It must have been very strange and difficult for them after our arrival, for Amma had until recently been the servant of the family. Now we were trying to serve her. Amma's material possessions were nil. Even the clothes that she wore were shared by her sisters. She would lie down on the sand when tired, even if it was raining. There was not even a mat for her, what to say of a pillow or a blanket. During the Bhava darshans, she would stand in the temple for more than twelve hours at a stretch. Packed with devotees, the temple had no air circulation at all and we had no fan. Yet Amma never complained about anything. She was the embodiment of renunciation and surrender. Whether pleasant or painful, she accepted whatever came as God's Will. She was and is an ideal in every way. Her life is an example to be followed by any serious spiritual aspirant, by any human being. She has said, "A true Master will always set an example for his disciples. A true Master, even though he is beyond all laws and limitations, must strictly adhere to moral and ethical values. Only then will he be an example to others. If the Guru says, 'Look, I am beyond everything, and therefore I can do whatever I like; simply obey me and do as I tell you,' this will only harm the disciple. A true Master will never do such things. All the great Masters of the past, the ancient saints and sages, were perfect, living examples of our highest and most noble values. Even if the Guru is beyond body-consciousness and devoid of all human weaknesses, the disciples are not. They are still identified with the body and the ego, and they therefore need a living example, an embodiment of divine qualities, to hold on to. The disciples draw all their inspiration from the Master. A true Master, therefore, places great importance on leading an exemplary life based on morality and ethics."

This was a blessed time for us, for there were many basic ways in which we could serve our Guru in the shape of food, clothing, something to sleep on and other minimal necessities. Amma accepted everything, not out of any need but to please us, to make it possible for us to serve her.

There is a story of a rich man who went to a temple and offered a bag of five thousand gold coins to the deity.

The priest there took the money as if it was nothing and gave it to the office. The man became disturbed. "Do you know that there are five thousand gold coins in that bundle?" he asked the priest. The priest nodded his head. "Are you sure you have understood what that means?" the man asked. The priest replied, "You have already said so. Am I so deaf that I didn't hear you?" The man piped up, "Listen, five thousand gold coins is a lot, even for a rich man like me." The priest looked at the man with pity and said, "Listen sir, are you asking me to be grateful to you, to give you a thank you?" "Well, at least that much is to be expected," said the man. "Wait a minute, sir. I will go and get the coins. You can take them back. You should be grateful that they have been accepted here. The giver should be grateful, for if the gift is not accepted, how can the giver benefit thereby?" asked the priest.

After about a month, it was decided that we would build a hut and live separately from the family. I had a little money and that sufficed to purchase the materials. Soon we had a hut, eighteen feet long and nine feet wide. Half of it was used as a kitchen and the other half served as a place for rest. Rest of course never meant slumber, for Amma rarely slept, and there would be people inside the hut meeting with her twenty-four hours a day. I don't remember ever seeing the light go off for the two years that we all lived together in that hut. At that time, Amma, Gayatri, Balu and I all stayed there permanently. This was the beginning of the ashram.

After two years, a devotee who occasionally used to visit Amma had another small hut built adjoining the first one. That became the first "guest house" of the ashram. Another one or two years later found two more huts constructed. These were used by the new residents, the brahmacharis who had come to stay. By that time, there were about ten or twelve of us. Yet, even though we all had a place to stay, there were many problems for which I wanted to find a solution. First and foremost was Amma's privacy and rest. Because Amma's room was a hut made of thatched leaves, people did not hesitate to call her from the outside or even look in between the leaves to see if she was there. No one cared to inquire whether she had rested or not, even after she had remained awake for many days and nights. They only cared about making their problems known to her and disregarded all else. Sometimes Amma would lie down at five or six in the morning after staying awake the whole night. Within ten minutes of her falling asleep, someone would come in from outside, bow down and touch her feet and call her until she woke up, just to tell her that they were going home! Seeing this happen again and again, I was at my wit's end to find a solution to the problem. But what could I do? It would have been nice to be able to build a regular room of bricks and mortar with real doors and windows so that Amma could have a little privacy. It would also have been nice for her to have a bathroom of her own, for she used to stand in line with the rest of us, waiting to use the bathhouse which consisted of a few coconut leaves placed around some stones to stand on. Our toilet was of the local type, a gunny bag stretched around four posts that were stuck in the backwaters with a few sticks as a "platform" for us to stand on. Those who come to the ashram now and feel a bit inconvenienced at not having a bathroom and toilet attached to their room might be well advised to remember what Amma and the first ashramites managed with for many years. What about a fan? The only fan in the ashram was an old "clunker" that served in the temple during the Bhava darshan, which we would afterwards put in Amma's hut to keep the sound of people's voices away so that Amma could get some rest now and then. We had scraped our pennies together in order to purchase it, for the heat in the temple was stifling in the summer. All of our water was carried from the village tap either by us or Amma's younger sister. This was no easy task, for the tap was a good fifty yards from the house and always surrounded by twenty or thirty ladies waiting for the water to come. This would usually happen around midnight or later.

Another problem was that none of the brahmacharis had a place to meditate. Most of the time they would have to vacate their huts to accommodate visitors, and they would rest under the trees. With frequent visitors coming at all hours, there was nowhere that one could go to meditate without disturbance. A meditation hall and a room for Amma became an utter necessity, but how would we get the money to build them? Amma strictly prohibited us from asking anyone for money for any reason. Because of this, we learned to depend on God for everything. This resulted in many interesting situations. There were times that Amma had to go out into the village with a begging bowl so that the brahmacharis could have something to eat. Once she sent Balu to his village to get some rice since we had no money to purchase any. Just as he was about to leave, a money order came by mail which enabled us to get a bag of rice.

I raised the idea of the construction and asked Amma about it. She absolutely refused unless we first built some kind of shelter for the visiting devotees. Strangely enough, different devotees soon donated bricks, sand, cement, wood and tiles, and we were able to build a decent hall for the visitors to sleep on darshan nights. Before Amma would retire into the hut, she would go around to each person and make sure that they were comfortable. There was not much we could offer them other than a space on the floor, but Amma's loving inquiries made them feel more comfortable than if they had been at home in a soft bed.

Now there was the possibility of building a room for Amma and a meditation hall for the ashramites. One day an idea flashed in my mind of going to America to try to collect some money for that purpose. At the same time, I fought against the idea of going, for I never wanted to leave Vallickavu or India as long as I lived. I felt that my spiritual good depended on that. Still, the idea kept coming to me again and again. However much I tried to suppress it, it would recur. I finally went to Amma and told her about my idea.

"Son, that idea is not yours, it is mine. The children need a place where they can meditate without disturbance. I did not want to tell you to go to America for that purpose because I know that you do not like going away, but there doesn't seem to be any other way. Go, but don't be disappointed if there is not a good response.

God will look after everything. We must do our duty, but the results are in His hands."

In preparation for the journey, I felt that I must have some kind of pamphlet about Amma's life. Until then, nothing had been written about Amma in any language. In fact, apart from stray facts that she mentioned now and then, none of us really knew anything about her life story. Now it became necessary to put that down on paper. Amma agreed to sit with us for some time every day in order to tell us about her life. But promises are made to be broken, as the saying goes. She would tell us a few things and then, becoming restless, would get up and go away. We asked questions in our efforts to piece together bits of information and to fill in gaps regarding details and dates. Everyone's patience was tested and tried, but finally we managed to write down most of Amma's life story.

One point remained unanswered, and it seemed that we would never pry it out of Amma. We wanted to know when she attained Realization. For some reason, she would avoid giving an answer when our "interrogation" reached that point. We tried many clever tricks, direct and indirect, to get an answer. First we directly asked her, "Amma, when did you attain Self-Realization?" She would immediately get up and go away saying, "This crazy girl doesn't know anything!" We then realized that the direct approach was not going to get us anywhere. Next, we asked her, "Amma, was it after the beginning of Krishna Bhava that Amma attained Realization or after Devi Bhava started?" We got the same answer—up and away! We then tried another technique. "Amma, is it possible for a person to show the Divine Bhavas before attaining Self-Realization?" But Amma was far more clever than we were, and would always avoid the issue. She knew well in advance what was going on in our minds and had made her plans long before we started in on the questions.

Finally, when I was about to leave, Amma admitted that she had realized her oneness with the Formless Brahman in her teens, before either of the Bhavas had started. It was after that she realized that all of the different aspects of God like Krishna, Ganesh, Shiva and Devi were within her. However, at the end of this admission, Amma said, "But, to tell the truth, the entire thing is only a *leela* (divine play)!" We were surprised and asked her, "Amma, do you mean that your sadhana, your Realization and the Bhavas are only a play?" "Yes, children," Amma said, "It has all been only to set an example for the world. Amma has never felt this universe to be real. From her birth itself she has felt the reality of God alone. The Krishna and Devi Bhavas are in Amma's hands. She can assume them whenever she wants. They are for the good of the world. Her innermost being is always the same, Eternal Peace." What more can be said? Amma's words speak for themselves.

The day of my departure arrived. I went to Amma to take leave of her, but she was in the temple getting some much needed rest. I simply bowed down at the temple door and left. I wanted to serve Amma and not have her serve me. I felt that it was more important that she rest than my seeing her and taking her leave.

After an uneventful journey, I arrived in America. My mother had offered to pay for the ticket and to help me in whatever way possible. Using the material that I had collected, we wrote a small pamphlet about Amma and sent it out to about a hundred and fifty people, appealing for help in Amma's work. I was not very hopeful. After all, I did not know anyone, and all of the people to whom we sent the appeal were friends of my mother. In fact, the response was very poor. I was disappointed and didn't know what to do. It was already almost two months since my arrival in America.

Then one day my mother said to me, "Neal, you know that when you left for India in 1968, I bought your coin collection from you so that you would have some money.

It is still with me. Why don't you take it and try to sell it?" I was very happy at this noble gesture and immediately started to investigate the coin collector's market. Within one week, I sold it for ten times as much as I had paid for it. This would be enough to build a room for Amma as well as a meditation hall. I immediately booked a ticket for India and before long, I was back with Amma.

Upon my return, Ganga, a brahmachari from France who had settled near Amma shortly after I did, sat down with me, and together we drew up a plan for the new building. I had a little experience with construction work from the days in Tiruvannamalai when I had two cottages built at the suggestion of my previous spiritual guide, Ratnamji. Ganga also had some experience from the same place; while in Tiruvannamalai, he had supervised some construction work for a Dutch devotee. We decided on a two-story building. The first level would consist of a single room and a small verandah which could be used for meditation, and there would be a little room under the staircase for storing tools. Upstairs there would be one room with a bathroom and porch for Amma's use.

Unfortunately, there was no land on which to build anything. All of the land we owned was occupied by our huts. If we were to remove them, where would we stay? We finally decided to fill in some of the backwaters which belonged to us. In order to get that much sand, it took quite some time, and so the work was delayed. Simultaneously, the old temple where Amma was holding the Bhava darshan, was being enlarged, so the darshan was held in the shelter that had been built for the devotees to rest in after the darshans.

Due to various difficulties, it took about one year to complete that small building. Obtaining materials, labor problems and water shortage all caused endless delays. For the same reasons, when a bigger building was constructed at a later time for devotees, what should have taken two or three years took seven. And even after the upstairs room was ready, Amma would not move in. Although Amma was beyond pleasure or pain, beyond comfort or a lack of it, she felt that she had to set an example of renunciation by continuing to live in the hut, despite the great inconveniences involved. It was two years after the completion of the building that Amma actually started to stay there at night. Eventually it became her quarters, and this occurred only because Ganga and I endlessly begged her to move in.

When one lives close to Amma, one is struck by her extreme concern for the spiritual improvement of the public. She prefers to suffer herself rather than set an anything less than perfect example. There is no need for Amma to follow any of the rules and regulations of spiritual life, for she is ever-established in the state which is the fruit of all such efforts. That is the state of an avadhuta, one who has transcended body-consciousness once and for all. Such people usually care little or nothing about the spiritual improvement of the world. They revel in their own state of Supreme Bliss and will not bother themselves about the suffering of others. In fact, they usually chase away those who approach them, pretending that they are mad, possessed or idiotic. To find a person established in God who is willing to sacrifice everything for the good of those whom they contact, is next to impossible. The number of such sages can be counted on one hand.

Some of Amma's householder devotees keenly desired to take Amma to Kanyakumari or Cape Comorin, the southernmost tip of India. A famous temple of the Divine Mother stands there where three different bodies of water meet—the Arabian Sea, the Indian Ocean and the Bay of Bengal—and the sand is of three different colors. An avadhuta lady, Mayee Amma, was living there, and we decided to spend some time in her company. Sunday night was Devi Bhava in Vallickavu, and so we left on Friday, planning to return by Sunday afternoon. There were about fifteen of us in a van.

On the way there, we stopped in a village named Marutamalai at the foot of a mountain of the same name famous for its herbal wealth. There was supposed to be an avadhuta living there as well; he was called Nayana. After making some inquiries, we found his hut, which was located on the main road. We all entered into the dimly lit room and found a very dirty old man sitting in the corner spitting red betel nut juice on the walls. We were told by one of the villagers that he had not taken a bath in more than ten years! That was easy enough to believe. Amma immediately sat down in front of him, but what was our surprise and anger when he slapped her on the face. Amma just looked at us and told us to calm down. He then spit in her face and shouted out in a language known only to himself. We naturally wanted to get out of there as soon as possible, but Amma was in no hurry. Finally, after twenty minutes or so, we left.

After sitting in the van, Amma turned to us and said, "Wonderful! He was in the Supreme State!" We could not believe Amma at all. The Supreme State? Supreme state of what? Madness? "None of you can understand. Only one who is in that State can recognize It in another," said Amma and kept quiet. We were all silently thinking, "If that is the Supreme State, I don't want it!"

We then proceeded to Kanyakumari, happy to leave Nayana alone in his Supreme State. After reaching the Cape, we sought out Mayee Amma who was staying by the ocean side. When we reached the place where she was, we found a very old, half-naked beggar-woman lying on the sand. She was using a dog as a pillow, surrounded by a pack of thirty or forty mongrels. Was this the great sage that we were looking for? If Amma had not told us that Mayee Amma was a Mahatma, it would have been impossible to believe who she was. She looked like a beggar of beggars. Amma sat down in front of her with all of us around her. Mayee Amma sat up and slapped Amma on the face. We were shocked! This was the second time in one day, in one hour, that Amma was slapped by a Mahatma. Amma simply smiled and climbed onto Mayee Amma's back and rode on her like a small child on its mother. Mayee Amma then got up and walked down to the beach. All of the garbage from the city of Kanyakumari had been collected and deposited there especially for her. Every day she would light a bonfire and perform a fire sacrifice, using the rubbish as the sacred offerings. What was the inner meaning of her mysterious life? No doubt only she and those in her state know. After finishing her "worship," she jumped into the sea stark naked and came up with a fish, which she proceeded to eat raw.

Amma as the Guru 125

Amma with Mayee Amma

Around noontime, a devotee of hers brought a tiffin carrier, a multi-tiered canister which contained her lunch. We all sat around her and sang devotional songs while she had something to eat. She then gave each person a little of her leftovers as a token of her blessing. One of the devotees who had come along with us was a very strict vegetarian from birth. To everyone except him, Mayee Amma gave vegetarian food, but to him alone she gave a piece of fried fish. And for me, she started to pour out some sweet pudding into my hands. But before it could reach my hands, a dog came and slurped it from the vessel as it was coming out. Whatever overflowed from the dog's mouth landed in my hands. Amma looked intently at me to see what I was going to do. I hesitated for a moment and then ate the pudding. When we go to Mahatmas, we should have full faith in their spiritual power. We should be ready to give up our attachment to all of our rules, regulations and conceptions. Then only will it be possible to get their blessing. Mayee Amma was giving us a chance to do just that.

After a more or less blissful two days at Kanyakumari, we got into the van to return to the ashram. As we approached Nayana's village, we all grew tense. We were afraid that Amma would want to stop to see him again. We were almost past the village when suddenly we saw Nayana standing in the road in front of the van, signaling us to stop. We all groaned. Seeing him standing there, Amma shouted for us to stop. She immediately jumped out of the van, followed by all of us. But Nayana was nowhere to be seen. Where had he gone? We made our way to his hut and found the door closed. Amma went inside first. There he was sitting in his usual corner. Even if he had run from the road to his hut, he could not have possibly reached his room in that short amount of time. Amma sat in front of him and we braced ourselves for the worst. Amma started to sway back and forth and began pinching Nayana on the leg. He simply sat there calmly, looking at her. Amma then closed her eyes; tear drops began to fall. We could not make out what was happening. Suddenly Amma exploded into *Kali Bhava*, the mood of Goddess Kali. Amma's tongue stuck out of her mouth almost down to her chin and she let out a terrific roar. Her eyes bulged and her hands manifested *mudras*. She started to bounce up and down like a ball and the bangles on her wrists got shattered to pieces. To say that we were surprised would be an understatement. After about ten minutes, Amma slowly returned to her normal self. When she opened her eyes, she looked like one fully intoxicated. Indeed, she was drunk with Divine Bliss.

Nayana then pointed at young Shakti Prasad, who had come with us, and said, "Your son, your son." Once again we were surprised, for all of us knew that Shakti Prasad had been conceived through Amma's grace. The fact that Nayana knew that Shakti Prasad was Amma's own child, proved to us that he was not as crazy as he appeared.

After getting into the van, Amma said, "On our way to Kanyakumari, Nayana understood who I was. He was waiting for me to come back because he wanted to see my real nature. That is why he manifested himself in front of the van and then disappeared. I understood that, and so when I sat in front of him, the urge to satisfy his desire arose in my mind. Seeing that divine mood of Kali, Nayana slipped into the mood of Shiva, and we enjoyed Transcendental Bliss together." The rest of the journey was comparatively uneventful and we reached the ashram just in time for the Devi Bhava.

The next day, Amma lay down in the sand outside the hut. Some time passed and she came inside and said to me, "Nayana Swami just came here to see me." I looked outside but didn't see anybody there. "No, no, I don't mean like that. He came in a subtle form and has now gone away." Living with Amma, one gradually realizes that this world which we see is not all there is to God's Creation.

One day a lady entered the ashram, walked over to one of the brahmacharis who was meditating in front of the temple, and blew some air into his ears. He was, of course, surprised. After doing this, the lady left. She had the appearance of a local villager. Amma saw her coming to and going from the ashram. She said that the lady must have been a Mahatma. I asked Amma why she thought so. Any crazy person could have acted in same the way. Amma said, "Otherwise, how could she have known that brahmachari has been suffering from abscesses in his ears? There are many such Mahatmas wandering around, unknown to the public."

Every morning we used to meditate for some time with Amma, sitting in the open space in front of her hut. One morning, I was late in joining the others. I quietly sat down about twenty feet away from Amma. Within a few seconds after closing my eyes, my mind became completely still. Then, in a little while, it again started its usual "monkey business." I sat there for about half an hour, got up and went into the hut. Amma entered the hut and said, "Son, did you have any experience in your meditation today? When you came and sat down near me, my mind turned towards you, took the form of Brahman, and went near you."

In the coming years, this became a sign for me that Amma was thinking of me. It happened many times, that even though far away from Amma physically, my mind would become still and an intense thought of Amma would occupy my consciousness. Sometimes, even while speaking to someone, this would happen, and I would have to stop talking and stand there like a silent fool. This gave me the faith that Amma's mere thought could bless me with the Realization that I sought. Amma had told me that this was indeed true. Four days after first meeting Amma, I returned to Tiruvannamalai. During the train ride I smelled various divine scents, felt as if Amma was right there with me, and experienced intense, frequent weeping and longing to see Amma. When I returned to her after a month and a half, I asked her about these manifestations. She confirmed what I thought to be true, that she had been thinking of me and that concentrated thought had blessed me with those experiences. What cannot be achieved even after years of spiritual practice can be gained in a moment through the thought or look of a Satguru, a Perfect Sage.

There is a beautiful story about a man who was a king in Persia. He was very fond of the spiritual way of life and always sought the company of saints. However, he lived in such luxury that he slept on a bed that was kept covered at all times by a twelve-inch layer of flowers. One day, when he was about to lie down, he heard a noise on the roof of the palace above his room. On investigation, he found two men roaming around up there.

"What are you doing here?" he asked them sharply.

"Sir, we are camel drivers and are searching for our lost camels," they replied.

Amazed at their stupidity, he said to them, "How do you ever expect to find camels on the roof of a palace?"

"O King, since you are trying to realize God in a bed of flowers, shouldn't we expect to find camels on a palace roof?" they replied.

This reply greatly shocked the king, and as a result of these words, he changed his way of life completely. He left his kingdom and went to India in order to find a Realized Guru. When he reached Benares, he heard about a Guru named Kabir. Going to his house, he asked him to accept him as a disciple.

Kabir said, "There is nothing in common between a king and a simple weaver like myself; two such different persons could hardly get on together."

But the king pleaded with him and said, "I have not come to your door as a king but as a beggar. Again I beg of you the boon which I seek." Loi, Kabir's wife, felt sympathy for the king and urged her husband to accept him. At last, Kabir acceded to her request.

The king was given the menial work of the house—cleaning the wool and thread, bringing water and firewood and other such jobs. Six years passed and the king did all the work without a murmur. One day, Loi entreated Kabir, saying, "This king has now been with us for six long years. He has been eating what we've offered him, and has been doing what we have ordered him to do, without uttering a word of complaint. He appears to be highly deserving of initiation."

Kabir said, "As far as I can see, the king's mind is not yet crystal clear." But Loi again entreated the saint, saying that she could not believe that he was unfit for initiation. "If you don't believe me," Kabir said to his wife, "you can prove it for yourself. The next time the king leaves the house, gather all the rubbish you can and take it to the top of the roof. When you see the king coming out to the street, dump the rubbish on his head. Then come and tell me what you hear from his mouth."

Loi did as she was told, and as the rubbish fell on the king's head, he looked up and sighed, "If this were Persia, you would not have dared do this to me."

Loi returned to her husband and told him what the king had said. "Didn't I tell you that the king was not yet fully deserving of initiation?" Kabir remarked.

Another six years passed during which the king worked just as hard as he had during the first six years. One day, Kabir said to his wife, "Now the vessel is completely ready to receive the gift." His wife said, "I do not find any difference between the condition of the king six years ago and now. He has been ever dutiful and willing and has never uttered a word of complaint, not even on days when there was not enough food to feed him." Kabir said, "If you want to see the difference, you may once again throw the rubbish on his head."

So the next day, when the king was passing the house, she did exactly as her husband had told her. The king looked up and said, "May you live long. This mind was still full of ego and self. It had to be treated this way."

Loi then went and told her husband what the king said. He called the king and gazed at him. By the power of Kabir's gaze, the king's mind went up and up and merged into the Supreme Being.

"Your sadhana is complete. Now you had better return to your kingdom," said Kabir.

Such is the omnipotent power of a Realized soul. One should seek out the company of a Guru and strive to get the Guru's Grace. If one attempts to do sadhana on one's own, a lot of precious time will be wasted in trying to reach the goal by trial and error. Even if one has a Guru, so many obstacles will arise from within and without. Why not get as much assistance as one can and reach the goal as quickly as possible? No matter how much one may study spiritual books and meditate, there will still be so many subtle aspects of spiritual life which one cannot possibly know how to meet. Saints who have walked on the path and have reached the goal are the greatest possible aid. Yet how rare they are.

While sitting with Amma one night in front of the temple, I asked her, "Amma, what must I do to realize God?"

Picking up a handful of sand, Amma said, "You must become like this sand. This sand allows everyone to step on it without complaining. It is the lowest of the low. Similarly, when you become nothing, at that very moment, you will become the All. Individuality must go. Only then can Universal Existence shine forth. This is the purpose behind all spiritual practice."

The word "mahatma" means great soul. Many spiritual aspirants have grandiose ideas of attaining great spiritual power and thereby become a mahatma. But what is a real mahatma? It is one who has destroyed the ego, one who has renounced his or her individuality and has thereby merged in the Universal Being. These alone are the marks of a great soul. These qualities do not exist in an egotist who seeks power. Only when one has conquered the ego does real spiritual power become accessible. God will not give His treasures to one who wants to maintain a separate identity.

One day a gentleman from Hyderabad arrived in Vallickavu. He said that he was a devotee of Devi and had been doing various sadhanas for many years in order to get the grace of the Divine Mother. He had heard about Amma and wished to sit in the temple during Devi Bhava and chant the *Devi Mahatyam*, an ancient and famous Sanskrit song in praise of the Divine Mother. Amma agreed to his proposal. That day after lunch Amma, Gayatri and I were resting under a tree. This gentleman also lay down under a tree about fifty feet away from us. About five minutes went by and Amma started giggling. She looked at us and said, "This man is an expert in black magic. He has memorized all sorts of mantras which enable him to control evil spirits which live on the subtle plane. With their help, he can create all sorts of mischief."

I was surprised to hear Amma say this and asked, "Amma, how can you say such a thing? You have hardly had time to observe him."

"I don't require any time to understand who is who. The breeze that has touched his body has carried those mantras here to me."

All my hair stood on end when I heard Amma's shocking words. I suddenly got a glimpse into Amma's world. I was speechless and my mind became paralyzed. Looking at Amma with our gross vision, how can we possibly understand who she is and how she perceives this world? We are living in a closed, dark room while Amma is standing outside in the bright, open space. Nothing is hidden from her vision. We are all familiar with the saying, "Nothing can be hidden from the all-seeing Eye of God." What is a mere expression for the average man becomes a living experience in the presence of a God-Realized Soul. If one lives in the company of such people, even for a short time, one will never again use expressions such as "God forbid," "God alone knows," or "God damn it," in a casual way. For the average person, God is only a word. That God exists is clearly known when one lives in the company of Mahatmas.

That night was Devi Bhava. Our friend, the black magician (for that was the name we gave him) came into the temple and sat down next to me. He had the book in his hand, ready to recite the Devi Mahatyam. But for some reason he became very restless and kept looking around on all sides. After fidgeting for about fifteen minutes, he finally got up and left the temple without reciting the song.

The next morning, he came to me and said that he had decided to leave that day. I asked him what was his hurry. He said that he still had to go to many places on his pilgrimage. I then asked him why he didn't recite the Devi Mahatyam the previous night, but he did not reply. I then felt a bit of mischief rising from within and asked him if he knew black magic. He turned pale and said, "No." I then repeated to him what Amma had told us about him. Hearing my words, he looked as if he was about to run out of the ashram, and then he said, "It is true that I studied those mantras a long time ago, but I never used them on anybody." Whether what he said was true or not, who could say, but I didn't want to make him any more uncomfortable, and so I asked if he would like to see Amma before he left. This probably made him even more uncomfortable because it was Amma who exposed him in the first place. Perhaps out of politeness he said, "Yes."

We then entered Amma's hut and found her sitting there talking to some devotees. Looking at him with a smile on her face, Amma said, "Son, how many children do you have and through how many women? Fifteen? Twenty? You should never use those bad mantras for any reason. Not only that; you should also not drink liquor and have illicit sex in the name of tantric worship. It will only lead to your downfall. You may think you are making some spiritual progress that way, but without the guidance of a Guru who has attained Realization through the tantric path, one will only damn oneself."

Hearing this, the man started to raise objections, but perhaps after a bit of reflection, he realized the truth of Amma's words and kept quiet. Bowing down to Amma, he left the place never to be seen again. About a month later, another man came from Hyderabad to see Amma. He told us that he was familiar with that gentleman who was indeed known for doing all those things which Amma had mentioned.

This incident made me wonder about the future fate of this man and others like him who are themselves deluded and who delude others as well. Will they not suffer after death or in a future life? This raised an even bigger question in my mind, whether or not there is any existence at all after the death of the body. Who would know better than she who had "died" for eight hours after her father had requested her in Devi Bhava to "give back" his daughter?

The next day, I asked Amma, "Amma, there is a story in the Upanishads about a boy who somehow traveled to the world of death and asked the Lord of Death, Yama, whether one continues to exist after the death of the body. Amma, you see all the worlds within your Self. Please tell me what happens after we leave the physical body."

Amma's expression became very serious and she said, "By asking about life after death, you are also asking about the doctrine of karma. Analyzing the law of karma is not so important. The most important thing is to get out of it, to go beyond the cycle of karma, which is caused by the ignorance about one's true Self.

"Negative actions committed in the past may not bear fruit in the immediate future, and the same is true with good actions. We may see a person lacking in virtue who lives a seemingly pleasant life, and we may see a good person suffering for no apparent reason. This may seem to contradict the law of karma; you may even decide that there is no such thing. However, to understand its significance, the law of karma needs to be examined and evaluated from a higher point of consciousness; and to be able to rise up and see karma from that higher level, faith and spiritual practice are required. Here the criterion is not the intellect but spiritual intuition.

"All of life moves in cycles; the whole universe is cyclic. Just as the earth moves around the sun in a regular cycle, all of Nature moves in a cyclic pattern. The seasons move in a circle: spring, summer, autumn, winter, spring again, and so forth. The tree comes from the seed, and the tree, in turn, provides seeds out of which new trees will grow. It is a circle. Similarly, there is birth, childhood, youth, old age, death, and birth again. It is a continuous circle. Time moves in a circle, not in a straight line. Karma and its results must inevitably be experienced by every living being, until the mind is stilled and one abides content in one's own Self.

"Cycles happen again and again as action and reaction. Time goes in cycles. It is not that the exact events happen over and over again; rather, the *jivatman* (individual soul) assumes different forms according to its *vasanas* (latent tendencies). Reactions are the results of actions performed in the past. It goes on and on. As the circle of life turns round, the actions of the past bear fruit. We cannot say when the fruit will come, what the fruit will be, or how it will come. It is a mystery known only to the Creator. You either believe in it or you don't. Whether you believe or not, the law of karma continues to operate, and the fruits come. Karma is without beginning, but it ends when one drops the ego, when one attains the state of Realization.

"Man evolves into God. Every human being is essentially God. Evolution from man to God is a slow process. It requires a lot of cutting, polishing and remolding. It needs a lot of work and requires great patience. It cannot be done in a hurry. Revolution is fast, but it kills and destroys. Man is revolutionary; God is evolutionary.

"The circle of life moves slowly and steadily. Summer comes; it takes its own time, it is never in a hurry. All the other seasons—autumn, winter, and spring—they all take their own time. Behind the mystery lies the invisible power of God. That power cannot be analyzed. Just trust that it is there.

"Try to forget about the cycle of karma. There is no need to think about the past; it is a closed chapter. Whatever is done is done. Confront the present. What is important is the present, because our future depends entirely on how we live in the present. Only when the presence of Divinity permeates every moment of our life, will we truly be in the present. Until then, we dwell either in the past or in the future. The present lies in this moment, but we always miss it. When we live in the moment, we are utterly here; the next moment doesn't matter. Living in the moment, in God, the Self, will stop the law of karma from operating in us.

"The power of karma veils our true nature, while at the same time, it creates the urge to realize the Truth. It leads us back to our real state of being. The circle of karma is a great transformer, if you have the eyes to really see. It conveys the great message: 'Your life is the effect of the past. Therefore, beware; your thoughts and actions in the present determine your future. If you do good, you will be rewarded accordingly, but if you commit mistakes or perform evil actions, those actions will return to you with equal strength.' And to the true spiritual seeker, there is this great message: 'It is better if you stop the circle completely. Close the account and be free forever.' All these explanations of karma serve to restrain humans from doing harm to themselves and to others, and to prevent them from moving away from their real nature, from God.

"Nothing is accidental. Creation is not an accident. The sun, moon, ocean, trees and flowers, mountains and valleys are no accidents. The planets move around the sun without straying even an inch from their predetermined orbits. The oceans cover vast areas of the globe, without swallowing up the entire earth. If this beautiful creation were an accident, it wouldn't be so orderly and systematic. The universe would be a chaotic mess. But look at the exquisite beauty and charm of creation, its intricate perfection. Can you call this an accident? The vast pattern of beauty and order that pervades throughout all of creation, makes it very clear that there is a big heart and an inconceivably great intelligence behind everything.

"Our past is not just the past of this lifetime. It is not just to be traced back to the birth of this present body. The past consists of all our previous lives, through which we have traveled in different names and forms. The future cannot be seen either; it is not under our control. We cannot predict what will happen tomorrow. The truth of karma is therefore more a matter of faith than anything else. Just as the waves of the ocean appear in different forms and sizes, the life force assumes various forms according to each one's accumulated tendencies.

"Once you realize the Self, you will know everything about karma. The mysteries of your previous births will also be revealed to you. You will realize the secret of the entire universe, of all of creation. Self-Realization alone will clear up the mystery. Once you attain Perfection, you will know that the real Self was and is ever-present. You will know that the true Self was never born nor will it die, and that it is never subject to the law of karma.

"There is no guarantee for the future, or even for the next moment. Death alone can be guaranteed. This moment is true; the next moment may bring death, who knows? A person who is thankful for everything, will let go of everything to lovingly embrace death with a smile. For such a person, death is beautiful; for him, death is not an enemy to be afraid of—on the contrary, death becomes his dearest friend. Death is not the end; it is the beginning of another life."

CHAPTER 6

Faith Through Grace

THAT SAME DAY A LETTER CAME from America from my brother Earl. He said that he would like to come and see Amma for himself, for I had told him about her when I had gone to America. Two weeks later he arrived. I showed him to my room which was nothing more than one part of the hut. He was a little surprised at my living conditions. He sat down on the bed and we started to talk. Just then, Amma came into the room and sat on the bed next to him. She looked him up and down and gave him a pinch on the arm, saying, "You're a little fat, aren't you?" For no apparent reason, Earl burst into tears. I thought Amma must have really given him a pinch, but it wasn't that. I had never seen him cry in my life. Amma looked over at me with a mischievous grin on her face. In the meantime, Earl was bawling like a child. Amma was very amused by his tattoos and scrutinized them thoroughly. They covered his arms and were all in "technicolor." There was a Krishna, a Buddha, the snake of *kundalini* and other spiritual subjects. He looked somewhat like a walking spiritual poster. The more he cried the more Amma smiled. Finally he gained a semblance of composure but couldn't say a word. Amma sat there for a few more minutes and then got up and left. He obviously just had the shock of his life. Such was Earl's first explosive meeting with the Divine Mother; yet further explosions were in store for him.

Earl asked me if I had any book about Lord Sri Krishna, and so I went and got the Bhagavatam from the ashram library. He spent a lot of his time reading it in my room, but each time he came across the word "Krishna" he burst into tears. As if this wasn't bad enough, he would also break down crying whenever he heard Amma's voice. As soon as he would get close to Amma during the Krishna Bhava, he would start to tremble uncontrollably and begin to cry. He would then come over to me and sit on the ground, hiding behind my *dhoti* (a cloth that Indian men wear from the waist down like a sarong). After going through this for a few days, he finally decided that he wanted to discuss the matter with Amma. I went into the next hut where Amma was staying, and asked her if I could bring him in, to which she nodded her approval.

After we entered Amma's room, she motioned Earl to sit next to her on her bed. I started to tell her that he had some questions to be clarified, but before I could say anything, he again burst out crying. Amma gave him a hug and looked knowingly at me with a big smile on her face. This went on for about ten minutes, after which I guess she stopped pressing his "crying button," feeling he had cried enough. He finally asked his question.

"I just want to say that I don't like it when I don't understand what's happening to me. After coming here, I seem to have developed some kind of mental weakness. Otherwise, why am I crying like this all the time?"

Amma graciously smiled and said, "In our heart of hearts we are all children of God, but as we get older, that child gets covered up by a hard shell formed by our evil actions. Lust, anger, jealousy, dishonesty, greed, pride and other such negative tendencies go to make up the shell. Finally, the soft little child becomes hard like a rock. But in God's presence or in the presence of a God-Realized soul, that shell starts to melt and crack, and thus a person begins to weep like a child. If that happens to someone, they are very lucky. Purity that cannot be achieved through many births of spiritual practice can be gained through a few moments of such weeping."

Earl was very happy and relieved to hear Amma's explanation. But after a few days his mind became skeptical again. Just before Krishna Bhava that night, he said to me, "I think all this weeping is due to some weakness of mine. Tonight I have decided that whatever may happen, I'm not going to break down crying." Such has been the resolute decision of many of Amma's children, but in the face of the tidal wave of her Divine Energy, the carefully constructed house of cards of the human ego can never remain standing.

Earl bravely entered the battlefield of Amma's temple and went up to her in Krishna Bhava. Sure enough, he didn't tremble or start crying. I had come into the temple to watch him meet with victory or defeat. Amma smiled at me as if to say that she fully knew of his plan from the moment of its conception. After having Amma's darshan, Earl came over and stood next to me with a look of self-confidence on his face. Seeing this, I went outside and sat down in front of the temple along with the other devotees. Soon after, Earl also came outside. But as soon as he stepped out of the front door, he suddenly stood up straight, and with a strange expression on his face, bolted for the rear of the ashram. Next followed such a loud and anguished cry that many devotees went rushing back to see what was happening. And who was there but Earl! Some of the devotees came back and asked what was wrong with my brother. Was he suffering from some kind of intense pain? I just smiled and said that I didn't know.

After the Krishna Bhava was over, I went to my room to take rest for a while. There was Earl sitting rather sheepishly, trying to read a book. I asked him if there was something the matter, and he replied, "You might have seen what happened in the temple tonight. I somehow controlled myself when I went for darshan. Although I started to weep, I was successful in suppressing it. Then I thought that I must have been right, that all this crying is just some kind of emotional thing. But the moment I reached the door of the temple, a tremendous current of energy started up from the bottom of my spine, and when it reached the top of my head, it exploded like a sky rocket. At that moment I became convinced that Amma is an Incarnation of God. Who else could have done such a thing to me?"

After a few days, Earl returned to America. He later told me that from that time onwards, not a day passed that he didn't burst into tears thinking of Amma. The following year, he came back to Vallickavu and approached Amma for her to bless him with getting a child, for his wife had not conceived for many years. Amma blessed him, and shortly after that, his wife did, in fact, become pregnant and gave birth to a very intelligent, precocious little boy. For the next two years, he came back to Vallickavu, bringing his wife and children. Finally, he decided to study law. He was already in his forties and to get a degree at that age is very difficult. When he asked Amma about it, she said, "There are a lot of obstacles in the way of your becoming a lawyer. But Amma will arrange it." During the course of his studies, it became doubtful as to whether or not he would pass his exams. He then wrote to Amma, requesting her once again to bless him so that he might pass the coming exams.

When I read the letter to Amma, she said, "He has become lax in his studies. Tell him to be more careful, and I will look after everything." The next time I saw Earl he told me that Amma had been absolutely correct and that after becoming more careful, he did not have any more problems in school. Ultimately, he got his degree and became a lawyer.

It is always inspiring to meet the devotees who come to see Amma and hear their stories of how they developed faith in her as the Divine Amma. There was an English professor who came regularly for Amma's darshan. When he was a young man, he had very strong spiritual tendencies. In fact, he even wanted to renounce the world and become a monk. But unfortunately, he was an only son, and if one is the only son in an Indian family, he is bound by duty to get married, have children and carry on the family line. The young man therefore agreed to get married and took a virtuous girl for his wife. The first night of their marriage he told his wife, "By God's will I was unable to lead the life of a monk and have thus gotten married. At least if one of my children is able to lead that kind of life, then I will be satisfied. Therefore, before sleeping with you, I request that you agree that our first child be dedicated to the Divine Mother and be put on the spiritual path." The girl unhesitatingly agreed to his wishes and some time after, gave birth to a son. Unfortunately, both of them forgot their vow, and their lives went on. As the years passed, their son developed a number of health problems, and many doctors were consulted but to little avail. Finally one day, they heard about Amma, whose village was just an hour or two from their village. By this time, the boy was already seven years old. The man therefore decided to make a trip to see Amma, hoping she could do something for his son. At the time of his arrival, the Devi Bhava had already started. He entered the temple and bowed down before Amma. When he raised his head, Amma smilingly asked, "Where is your son? Why didn't you bring him to Me? Don't you remember the promise you made to offer your first child to Me on the night of your marriage?" Needless to say, he was shocked and henceforth developed deep faith in Amma as the Divine Mother Herself.

Animals also had a role to play in the events at the ashram. One night during the Devi Bhava, one of the ashram calves started to make a loud bellowing noise and sounded as if it was very sick. All of us, with the exception of Amma who was sitting in the temple, went to see what was the matter. We found the calf lying on the ground in convulsions. There was not much that we could do, so we reported the matter to Amma. As soon as the Devi Bhava was over, Amma came running to the cow shed and took the calf's head onto her lap. She told somebody to bring some holy water from the temple, and upon receiving it, she poured it into the calf's mouth and made a sign with her hands as if to say, "Now, you go." Within a few moments the calf breathed its last. Amma turned to us and said, "This calf was a sannyasi in its previous birth. Somehow he developed an attachment for a cow, and as a result, he was reborn as a cow. But because he was a monk, he was born in this ashram and received the benefit of the holy company of devotees and saints. He was blessed by the sound of the chanting of the Divine Name and was fed by the hands of spiritual aspirants. Now he has attained a higher birth." Such are the mysterious workings of karma. Hearing Amma's explanation, the little sadness we had on the sudden demise of the calf vanished. Amma later told us that her own mother should have passed away that night. In fact, earlier the same day she had told her mother to prepare for the worst. Amma said that she decided to extend her mother's life by transferring her death to the calf and thereby fulfill the calf's karma as well. Amma also told us that she had done the same for hundreds of people who had come to her over the years. She saw that their time for departure was near and that their death would create tremendous difficulties for their families, and so, out of compassion for them, she extended their lifetimes. She would ask them to purchase a cow, a chicken and a dog or cat, and then on the fated day these animals would die instead of them. Hearing this, we came to realize that not only is Amma's own life and death in her hands, but so are the lives of her devotees.

One evening I was standing outside talking to Sreekumar. He suddenly screamed and fell down. Looking at his foot, we found two marks which looked exactly like a snake bite. Immediately we rushed over to Amma and told her what had happened. She came running to Sreekumar, took his foot in her hands, sucked the poison from the bite and spat it out. Gradually his pain increased, and by night it was unbearable. Amma sat with him the whole time, comforting him and telling him there was nothing to worry about. But the other devotees felt that he should be taken to a doctor and be treated for poisoning. Amma gave her consent and they took him away. When the doctor saw the wound and the other symptoms, he told the devotees that Sreekumar had been bitten by an extremely poisonous snake, but strangely enough there was no sign of poison in his blood. He returned to the ashram that night in excruciating pain which decreased only by the next day.

Amma explained to him, "Son, you were destined to be bitten by a snake yesterday wherever you might have been. Yet because it happened in Amma's presence, no harm came to you. Knowing that this was going to happen, I did not allow you to go home yesterday, even though from morning onwards, you were requesting me to allow you to go." When Sreekumar looked at his horoscope upon reaching home, he did indeed find that he was to suffer from poisoning on that very day. Thinking of Amma's grace, he was overwhelmed with emotion and wept at the thought of her compassion.

One may ask why Amma did not simply prevent Sreekumar from being bitten by a snake since she knew that it was going to happen. Amma says that after surrendering to God or a God-Realized Guru, one's karma is greatly attenuated, but one will still have to suffer a little. To demonstrate this point, she tells the following story.

"There once lived a wealthy landowner with two sons who by nature were opposites. The boy named Mohan was inclined towards all that was evil, while the boy named Sasi was noble and religiously inclined. When they grew up, Mohan indulged in wine, women and gambling, whereas Sasi immersed himself in religious activities and would go to any religious gathering in the nearby villages. Mohan mocked his family's spirituality. He felt that it was his misfortune to have been born into such a family.

"One day there was a dance performance in the neighboring village by a famous dancing girl. Mohan was to be the patron and special guest. He was welcomed as a rich man's son. The same evening there was a religious discourse going on in the same village and Sasi went to hear that. On his way back, there was a heavy downpour, and he slid into a ditch and severely hurt himself. He was carried home by his friends and a doctor was called to treat him.

"Mohan, after enjoying himself with the dancing girl and her party, started on his way home and slipped at the same place. But Mohan did not fall. His foot struck a big stone. Looking closely, he found that it was a bar of gold. Rejoicing, he came home with it and showed it to everyone. Seeing his brother's pitiful condition, he taunted him saying, "What is the use of your religion? You went to hear the scriptures recited and on your way home you have met with a terrible accident. Look at me. I had a good time and have been rewarded with a bar of precious gold. When will you give up your old-fashioned way of life? If there is a God, He surely would have punished me and rewarded you, yet what do we see?" An argument ensued among the people present but no conclusion was reached as to who was right, the rationalist or the believer.

"The next day a Mahatma was passing through the village. The father of the boys invited him to their house. He told the Mahatma what had happened and what Mohan had said. The question was, why should a religious-minded boy get hurt and an evil-minded fellow be rewarded? The Mahatma said, 'The night of the incident, Sasi was destined to die. Because of his devotion and innocence, he was only hurt. That same night, Mohan was destined to attain a position of royalty, but due to his evil deeds, what he got was only a bar of gold. If you do not believe me, look at the boys' horoscopes.' When the horoscopes were consulted, it was found that the words of the saint were correct."

Sometimes a thousand or more people would come to the ashram on Bhava darshan days to see Amma. Amma would sit in her hut from morning until afternoon receiving everyone, and then again at night she would give darshan to each one, once during Krishna Bhava and again during Devi Bhava. In those days, the Krishna Bhava would go from seven in the evening until midnight. After that, Amma would come outside and sit with the devotees for half an hour before giving darshan in Devi Bhava, sometimes until six or seven in the morning. After that, she would meet with the devotees and sit with them until eleven o'clock. Then the young men who were later to become brahmacharis would arrive, one after another, and Amma would spend the rest of the day with them. At night she would usually be invited to do *puja* (worship) in the houses of devotees who lived in the nearby villages. Usually the puja would start around midnight and go on until three or four in the morning, and when it was over, Amma would sit with the devotees until the sun rose before coming back to the ashram. Then the same routine would repeat itself, sometimes going on like this for ten days at a stretch. It was impossible for any of us to keep up with Amma's pace, for didn't we need some sleep? We also felt that she needed some sleep and tried various tricks to lure her into taking some rest. We had a noisy old fan which would shut out all other sounds with its racket, and this became an effective means of insulating Amma from the surrounding world. Even after lying down, if she heard a human voice, she would jump up to see if it was someone who had come to see her. The scriptures say that the state of Self-Realization is that wherein the small self ceases to exist and the glory of selfless existence shines forth. Amma's life is a living commentary on this saying. One must see it to believe it. On certain days when many visitors arrived unexpectedly, the ashram residents would give their own food to them. And then what would Amma do? She would take a big pot and go from door to door in the village, begging for any left-over rice in order to feed us. She would say, "A sannyasi should have no bashfulness. Nor should a mother be ashamed to beg for her children's sake." Amma shows us through such actions not only what real detachment is, but also what true love is. If ordinary family life is led in a selfless manner, even there one may make spiritual progress. There is a nice story to illustrate this point.

At one time there was a severe famine. A family of five left their home in order to find a livelihood elsewhere.

The father underwent many hardships and privations in order to feed his family, and many days he had to starve. As a result, he died after a short while. Now the mother had to assume the responsibility of looking after the children, and she, in turn, underwent extreme privations and became debilitated to such an extent that she could no longer walk. Seeing her condition, her young son said, "Amma, please rest and I will go begging for all of us." She felt very miserable at the thought that her son had to take to a life of begging in order to obtain their food, but what choice did she have? He went for many days without food so that the rest of the family could eat.

Some days passed and the boy became so weak that he too could hardly walk. Somehow he reached a house and asked for a little money. The owner of the house was sitting on the verandah and offered to give the boy some food instead. At that point, the boy fainted. The man picked up the boy and sat him on his lap. The boy was murmuring something. The man put his ear to the boy's mouth and listened closely. The boy said, "The food that you wish to give, please give it first to my mother." After uttering these words, the boy became unconscious.

This kind of familial love does not exist nowadays. Look at the noble affection that bound these souls together in selfless love. When family life is led in this way, it purifies the family members' minds and leads the way to Liberation.

There is a misconception in the minds of many people, particularly in India, that only a monk can realize God. Yet over the years I have met some married devotees who are far more advanced than many sannyasis that I have seen. In the days when I was visiting Hyderabad in Andhra Pradesh, I became close to a married devotee there. He had started his spiritual life when he was in his mid-forties, and by the time he passed away in his late seventies, he had realized God. He did not, however, have an easy time of it, but then who does? Every morning he would get up early, worship God, do his mantra *japa* (repetition) and read the scriptures. In the evening also, when he came back from work, he would do the same. During the day he would repeat the name of God continuously. If he could find any saint living in the city, he would invite him to his house and keep him there as long as the saint wished to stay, treating him like a king the entire time. In addition to this, he would arrange religious festivals in his house, which would sometimes last a whole week. His surrender to God's will was also exemplary. One day I accompanied him to a hospital to visit another devotee who was ailing. As he sat on a

Faith Through Grace

chair by the devotee's bed, a nurse came by, wheeling a curtain on a metal frame. Somehow it tilted and fell on top of him, the frame hitting him on the head. He fell down on the ground and was stunned for a moment. I was afraid that he had been severely injured, but the next moment he got up and laughing said, "Thank you very much, O God, thank you very much." He had a number of physical problems which made it almost impossible for him to travel, yet when duty called, he unhesitatingly went where he was required. He had started off as a wealthy man, but due to the greed of his relatives, he had lost everything. They used to send all of their children to him to be educated and fed at his expense. He accepted everything as coming by God's will for his spiritual development and unconditionally surrendered. If a married person can continuously engage his mind in the thought of God through mantra japa, scriptural study, worship, renunciation, the company of saints and sages, humility and surrender to God's will, they can surely attain Realization. Whatever may be one's station in life, intense effort is needed. But what usually happens is that man gets distracted by the many attractive objects of the world and remains stuck to the earth. Such is the power of Maya, the universal illusion of the Lord.

Once there was a very virtuous king, yet he had no children. As old age approached, he became more interested in spiritual pursuits than in worldly affairs and spent much of his time in scriptural study, japa, meditation and *satsang* (holy company). The ministers of the government felt worried that there would not be a suitable heir to the throne if the king were to die before nominating someone. They therefore approached him and expressed their fears.

The king told them, "Don't worry. I shall choose a worthy successor." The king thereupon asked them to construct a fairground full of wonderful stalls of various kinds, so alluring and tempting that only the most steadfast, detached and persevering individual would be able to resist them. There were game booths, theaters, artificial ponds and parks, bakeries and other places of amusement and pleasure. The king then had an announcement made that he was preparing to choose an heir. Whoever could find the king in the midst of the fair would be chosen as the next king.

Thousands of people came, and all but a few were so attracted by the alluring sights, music and delicious food that they forgot all about the purpose of their being there and became immersed in enjoying themselves. Those few who did not fall prey to these temptations tried to find the king, but after a while, they too felt that the effort involved was so strenuous that it was better to spend their time in the pleasures of the fair.

Four days passed and no one had yet found the king. On the fifth day a bright young man entered the fairgrounds. Though he admired the fair, he did not allow himself to get distracted or to lose sight of his goal, and headed straight for the temple in the middle of the grounds. He entered the temple but did not find the king. He thought that if the king was in the fairgrounds at all, he would be in the temple. He went around the temple but could not find him. He then looked closer and found a small door in the side of the temple. He entered the passage and came to the other end. There was another door there which he opened. Suddenly, a brilliant light streamed out from the innermost chamber and there in the center of the room, seated on a throne, sat the king. The young man bowed down before the emperor who sat there smiling. At last, a worthy heir to the throne had been found.

This world with its many attractions is the fair and God is the king. He has sent us here not just to enjoy the objects of the world but to find the Lord hiding within them. Even though we are His children and heirs to His kingdom, yet we can gain that only if we seek Him with steadfastness, patience and perseverance without allowing our senses to distract us from the goal. We can enjoy what comes our way without attachment and thereby pierce through the veil of illusion which conceals God from our sight. Whether one is a monk or a householder, the world and its distractions will be there and must be overcome if one wants to succeed in spiritual life.

It was sometime in April of 1985 that the construction of a guest house and temple became an utter necessity. For a long time there already had been a continuous flow of visitors to the ashram. Because there was no accommodation for them, the brahmacharis would vacate their huts and sleep outside. This would not have been a problem if it happened only now and then, but it had become continuous and was therefore a disturbance to their spiritual practice. In addition to this, the small Bhava darshan temple could not contain all of the devotees at one time. Amma wished that everyone could sit with her during Devi Bhava (she had already discontinued Krishna Bhava by this time), and that would be possible only if the darshan took place in a huge room. Therefore, it was decided that a building combining both rooms for visitors and a temple for the Bhava darshan should be constructed. A well-to-do devotee purchased the land in front of the existing ashram and it was on that spot that the building was to come up. Amma asked me and another devotee of hers who was an architect to draw up rough plans independently. When we got together after a few weeks, what was our surprise to find that we both had the same identical plan. We came to the conclusion that the plan was Amma's and that we were only her instruments. Now the problem was money; where were we to get the funds required to build such a big building? The total area was to eventually come to thirty thousand square feet. Amma told us that we need not ask anyone for anything. If God wanted to build the building, he would supply everything necessary for it. Shortly after this, four or five of Amma's Western devotees offered donations so that the work could begin. But after some time we ran out of funds. The two houses that I had constructed in Tiruvannamalai were sitting there vacant. I offered to sell them, but Amma was not inclined to agree. Perhaps she was testing me to see if I had any attachment to my old haunt, but I had long ago ceased to think of Tiruvannamalai and my life there, as I had completely dedicated myself to serving Amma. I persisted in pestering her to allow me to sell them, and she finally agreed. In this way, somehow or other, we continued to build.

Amma felt that she and the ashram residents and visitors should take part in the construction work. She said that by doing so we could develop a more compassionate outlook towards the suffering of those who lead hard lives. Such heavy work would also be good for our health and we could save some money besides. Since it was for a spiritual purpose, this work would also be *karma yoga* (desireless action to please God). Therefore, Amma, along with everyone else, started carrying loads of earth from the foundation pit. After that, everyone carried stones, sand, cement, bricks, wood and other building materials to the site and also took part in the concrete work. I wondered how many other Self-Realized sages in this world have spent a good deal of their time doing heavy work like this to set an example for others.

It was also around this time that Amma began to travel extensively throughout India at the invitation of her many devotees. She went to all of the major cities of India, Bombay, New Delhi, Calcutta, Madras as well as many smaller towns and villages in Kerala itself. In each place the reception was overwhelming; often tens of thousands of people came to see her. Amma would sit sometimes for six or eight hours at a stretch, giving darshan until every last person was seen. Due to these frequent travels, devotees in the different places that Amma visited undertook to start ashram branches so that Amma's programs could be held therein. At other times, these would become a source of solace for those who could not come to Vallickavu to see Amma.

CHAPTER 7

Going Abroad

ONE DAY I RECEIVED A LETTER from Earl, saying that as he was in the midst of his studies, he could not possibly come to India for a few years. Would Amma consider coming to America instead? He said that the money that he would have to spend on his ticket could be used to purchase a ticket for Amma's journey to the United States and back. I took the letter and went to Amma and read it to her. She said, "Tell him Amma will come. You arrange everything." At that time there were only two Americans staying at the ashram; I was one and the other was a young woman, Kusuma, who had been staying there for some months. I thought it over and decided that after eighteen years in India, I was not prepared to arrange Amma's foreign tour. I therefore asked Kusuma if she was willing to try. She agreed, and Amma also approved; and within a few days she left for the States. After discussing it with Amma, we decided that since Amma was going to travel half-way around the world anyhow, she might as well complete the journey back to India through Europe. Going to America and some European countries, Kusuma contacted as many people as she could, met with a favorable response to Amma's proposed visit, and returned to India, reporting everything to Amma and to me. Amma then asked her to go once again to make all the arrangements, which she did.

It was decided that Amma was going first to Singapore, then to San Francisco, Seattle, Santa Fe, Chicago, Madison, Washington D.C., Boston and New York. From there she would go to France, Austria, Germany and Switzerland, and then return to India. The entire tour would take three months. I asked Amma if the ashramites were going to be able to bear her being away so long. She replied that Amma's absence would give them a chance to do more introspective spiritual practice and to develop real longing for God, for living with Amma was something like a continuous festival, and one even tended to forget that the whole purpose of being with her was God-Realization. One may wonder how such a thing could be possible, that is, how one could forget the real purpose of being with Amma.

In the ancient days, the Lord incarnated in North India as Sri Krishna. His life story is related in the holy scripture, Srimad Bhagavatam. It is stated therein that the purpose of the Lord's incarnation was to destroy the wicked and to protect and inspire the good. It was for the purpose of becoming an object of devotion for the present and for future generations that the Lord assumed a most charming personality, though in essence He is beyond all form or quality. This is one of the distinguishing features of the ancient religion of India, for one of the tenants is that the Supreme Being incarnates at regular intervals whenever dharma is on the decline. When He incarnates, He causes a tidal wave of devotion and spirituality to flood across the world. He plants in the hearts of human beings an irresistible fascination for Him alone, so that they are effortlessly drawn to His Divine Presence and want to remain there only. The Gopis, milkmaids who lived in the same village as Krishna, experienced this tremendous attraction from the time of His birth. Whatever they did, they could think only of Krishna. Even when they were going through the streets selling their goods, they called out, "Krishna! Kesava! Narayana! (names of Krishna)" instead of "Milk! Butter! Yogurt for sale!" From the moment Krishna left the village to graze the cows until the time He came back in the evening, the Gopis' minds were dwelling on Him. They didn't do meditation or any other spiritual practice, yet they achieved the highest state of identification with God. How was this possible? The Bhagavatam says that we can realize God by constantly thinking of Him, no matter what the attitude towards Him may be. We can love Him as our own child, as our husband, as our beloved, as our friend, as our relative; or we can hate Him as our arch enemy, or be afraid of Him. Through all these ways, we can realize Him through constant remembrance, for that is the criterion for God-Realization. Constant remembrance is in itself meditation, for what is meditation but one-pointed remembrance of one thing to the exclusion of all else. Of course, one would not want to think of God through hatred or fear because it is painful to be the enemy of God. To attain Realization, it is not enough, in fact, to merely meditate a few times a day, forgetting God the remainder of the time. Constant remembrance at all times is the basic requirement for a successful spiritual life; therefore, the thought of God must permeate all our daily activities.

Living with Amma is like living with Krishna. Her devotees' minds are inexplicably drawn to her. A unique happiness is felt in her presence; yet Amma says that to maintain that feeling always, spiritual practices in the form of mantra japa, meditation, and self-control are needed. While one may be spontaneously peaceful and happy in

Amma's presence, one may not think about how it will be in her absence. This is why Amma thought that a three-month separation, however unpleasant, would be good for her children's spiritual growth. Apparently they had reached a level of sufficient maturity that they were ready to avail such an opportunity. It is actually the experience of many of Amma's devotees that their concentration and devotion are of greater intensity when they are far away from her than when they are in her physical presence. Separation is indeed a very effective means to increase longing. In the lives of the Gopis, this is exactly the way that Krishna effected their Realization.

One full moon night, Lord Krishna blew on his flute as a signal for all the Gopis to come running to the forest to meet him for the famous *Ras Leela* (dance of bliss). This dance is symbolic of the divine bliss which the soul enjoys in union with God. Leaving their homes and families, the Gopis came running to the forest where they danced in bliss with their Beloved Krishna. After the Gopis' meeting with the Lord, they became a little proud of their good fortune, and at that moment Krishna disappeared. Immediately they became mad with longing to see him again, and they wandered through the forest in a frenzied search. As their madness reached its peak, the

Lord reappeared in their midst and soothed their agony. They asked Him, "Some love in return those who love them, while others do just the reverse. They love even those who do not love them. Still others do not love either. Kindly explain this to us clearly, O Lord." In other words, the Gopis were accusing the Lord of indifference towards them, even though they were overflowing with love for Him. They wanted to know why He acted in such a callous way.

Krishna replied,

> "They who love one another for mutual benefit, O friends, really love their own self and none other, for their endeavour and deed is solely actuated by self-interest. Neither goodwill nor virtue play any part there, for such a love has a purely selfish motive and not otherwise. They who actually love even those that do not love them in return are compassionate and loving, like one's parents. There is blameless virtue as well as goodwill operating here, O charming girls. Some indeed do not love even those that love them, much less those that do not love them. They are either sages, revelling in their own Self and have no perception of duality, or those who have realized their ambition and are therefore free from craving for enjoyment, though conscious of external objects,

or dullards who are incapable of appreciating a good turn done to them, or ungrateful people who bear enmity to their own benefactors, though conscious of their services. I, for my part, O friends, do not come under any of these categories, inasmuch as I do not visibly reciprocate the love of even those individuals who love Me, in order that they should ever think of Me in the same way as a penniless person would, on a treasure found by him being lost, remain engrossed in the thought of that wealth alone and would not be sensible to anything else. Indeed, in order to insure thus, your constant devotion to Me, O fair ones, I remained out of your sight for some time, though loving you invisibly and listening to your professions of love with great delight, you, who have for My sake, ignored all worldly decorum as well as the injunctions of the scriptures and deserted your own people. Therefore, O beloved ones, you ought not to find fault with Me, your darling. I can never repay my obligation to you, whose relation with Me is absolutely free from blemish and who have fixed your mind on Me, completely cutting asunder the fetters that bound you to your home and which cannot be easily be broken."

—Srimad Bhagavatam X, 32, v.16-22

From these words of the Lord, we can see how the physical separation from a Divine Being serves to purify us and fix our minds irrevocably on God. While Krishna was leaving Brindavan, the place of His childhood, He told the sorrowing Gopis that He would come back soon, but in fact, He never did. It was only many years later that He met them again in Kurukshetra where people from all over India assembled during an eclipse of the sun. By that time, the Gopis were so full of the thought of Krishna and so perfectly surrendered to His will, that their individuality had merged into His Being. Their turbulent longing and devotion had given way to the perfect peace of Unity. This is the final fruit of devotion to God. What was true of Krishna and the Gopis will be true of any Divine Soul and their devotees. It is for the above reasons that Amma felt that a three-month separation would be good for her children who had been enjoying her constant company, some of them for many, many years.

It was decided that some of us should go to America on a pre-tour in order to introduce Amma to the people before her arrival. Therefore, two other brahmacharis and I left about two months before Amma on March 22, 1987. We went to Singapore, and after staying there for

Going Abroad

three days of introductory programs, we proceeded to San Francisco. This was the first time that the brahmacharis were going outside of India and it was a novel experience for them. I became their "Westernizing-guru," even though I myself was in a state of culture shock. Just as Westerners feel shocked when they go to India—for it takes them some time to adjust—people coming from India also feel the same when they come to the West. Though on the same earth, India and the West are worlds apart. We all stayed in Oakland at the house of my brother who was studying at the time for his law degree in Berkeley. Accompanied by two other devotees, we travelled in a battered old Volkswagen van to all the places that Amma was to visit. We gave talks about Amma and sang devotional songs in each place. We were surprised to find so many people who would start crying while hearing about Amma or listening to the singing. It seemed that Amma already had many children here. We went as far as New York and then came back to San Francisco to receive Amma.

Upon our return to my brother's house, we phoned Singapore to find out whether Amma had actually reached there, for it was, in a way, unbelievable to us that she would leave India, even though that was indeed the plan. How would the ashram residents survive her absence? What must have been the scene when she left? Perhaps, seeing their sorrow, she had cancelled the trip. In that case, we had better go back to India. These were our thoughts at that time. But we were relieved of our anxiety when Gayatri picked up the phone and told us that everyone had arrived safely. Just then, Amma took the phone and shouted, "Children!" The three of us and the phone all fell on the floor, and the two brahmacharis burst out crying. After a moment, they picked up the phone and asked, "Amma, you will be coming here, won't you?" Amma reassured them and after talking for some time, said good-bye. The brahmacharis had been away from Amma for nearly two months, and this had been a great emotional strain for them. Hearing Amma's affectionate voice burst the dam of their hearts.

Two days later on May 18th, Amma arrived at the San Francisco Airport in the afternoon, where a large crowd had gathered to receive her. Amma was just like a child, looking around at everything, waving to everybody and giving affectionate hugs to all who came near her, even those who hadn't come to see her at all! We drove to Earl's house together in a rented van and told Amma about everything that had happened during our pre-tour. She also related to us what had happened at the ashram during

Going Abroad

Amma's arrival at San Francisco Airport, 1987

our absence. Upon reaching the house, Amma immediately sat to give darshan. We were extremely worried, because Amma had just been sitting in an airplane for more than sixteen hours and must have certainly been exhausted. Now she was going to sit for another two or three hours to meet her Western children. We protested, but Amma would hear nothing of it. She said, "These children have been waiting a long time to see me. What does it matter if I take rest only after a little while? I have not come here to be comfortable; I have come to serve the people."

Amma's daytime darshans and night time programs were well attended. The daytime darshan was held in Earl's house while the night programs were in different churches and halls in San Francisco, Berkeley, and Oakland. Amma also spent a few days in Santa Cruz and Carmel. In the evenings, there was generally a short talk, followed by devotional singing led by Amma, and then darshan until midnight. The first Devi Bhava in the Western world was held inside Earl's house. It was a thrilling experience for everyone. The Western devotees did not know what to expect, and neither did we! Earl's house filled up and the crowd started to overflow into the streets. Everybody was crushed into the room adjacent to the Devi Bhava hall, and people were literally climbing on top of each other to see what was going on. It looked like a madhouse. People had heard that Amma was going to go into some kind of trance, and nobody wanted to miss seeing that. Before the darshan began, everyone was singing, or rather, screaming the Divine Name.

Finally, the doors to the "temple" opened and pin drop silence prevailed. The looks on the faces of the people cannot be described. They drank in Amma through their eyes like people who had been dying of thirst. Never before had they seen such splendour and majesty, as if the Queen of the Universe had descended to grace human beings with a glorious vision. The brocaded silk sari she wore shimmered as she vibrated with divine energy, and the jewels on her crown emitted beams of light like the rising of a thousand suns. One by one, people lined up to receive darshan with the Goddess who had come to earth, while the air was filled with singing. The darshan continued until three or four the next morning. When I was cleaning the room afterwards, I found that many of the sheet rock walls had formed cracks due to the pressure of the crowd packed inside. It was fortunate that the building hadn't collapsed! Amma had certainly come to America with a bang!

During the tour, Gayatri would cook lunch for all of us in the daytime and keep a portion of it aside for supper because, by the time we returned from the night time programs, it was always too late to cook. Unfortunately, while we were still staying at Earl's, some of the devotees, attracted by savoury smells in the kitchen, discovered how tasty Indian food is and helped themselves to our supper. When we came back after midnight, what was our surprise when we found that somebody had been "eating our porridge." In order to save the day, I went to the local Safeway Supermarket and bought two loaves of bread and some jam, and we all helped ourselves. As we were eating, Amma walked in and asked why we were eating bread instead of rice. I explained to her what had happened.

"How much did this bread and jam cost?" asked Amma.

"About four dollars," I said.

"Four dollars! That's nearly fifty rupees in India. Do you know how many people can be fed for fifty rupees? If you had purchased four dollars worth of rice and vegetables and spent an extra half an hour cooking, you would have had something left over for tomorrow as well. Just because you're in America doesn't mean that you should stop calculating in rupees."

When Amma was a child, she suffered from extreme poverty. She was treated as a servant by her family. She often went many days without food and was given clothing of the cheapest type. She would make do with whatever was available, stitching and re-stitching her torn clothes time and again. Even after the ashram came into existence, she remained extremely economical. She tried to impress upon us that everything was given to us by God and was therefore valuable and deserving of great care. Just because she had come to the affluent West, she wasn't about to change her principles, nor will she ever.

Many enlightening conversations took place during Amma's tour. During one daytime satsang, someone asked, "Amma, the scriptures say that I am the *Atman* (Self). If that is so, why should I meditate and do other preparatory purification, rather than just dive into that Reality?"

Amma replied, "Child, if that were possible for you, then why are you asking the question? Even though you have heard that you are the Atman, you cannot say that you are able to enjoy being That, nor can you see everything as That. Only if you plant the seeds and raise the plants will you be able to enjoy the flowers.

"If you have never actually seen your father, you will not be satisfied by merely hearing his name. You must actually see him. Similarly, if you miss your mother when she is staying somewhere far away, you will be happy only after going there and seeing her. One will attain bliss only through the direct experience of the Atman, not through the mere intellectual knowledge that it exists. At present, we have only an intellectual conviction that Truth exists. Like a monkey, our mind jumps restlessly here and there, and with such a mind it is difficult to reach the Eternal. If a cat gets a taste of fish, it will not be at peace until the fish has been eaten. In a similar way, when our mind comes in contact with the world, it becomes uncontrollable like the restless monkey or the hungry cat.

"Even though we may know that the Supreme Reality lies within us, we still act as though happiness can be gained from the material world. Due to this attraction to the objects of the world, we are unable to make much progress towards Realization. Suppose you place an inkwell on the right side of your desk and use it for ten days. Even if you move it to the left side, on the eleventh day your hand will automatically go to the right side. Old habits pull us down and do not allow us to progress spiritually.

"Children, in order to train the mind to stop running from object to object, we must cultivate new habits like meditation and mantra japa. By doing so, we will gain concentration. Just as we dam a river and channel the water in order to produce electricity, the effect of doing spiritual practice is to direct the different wanderings of the mind to a single point, thereby making it subtle and powerful. Without achieving this state of concentration first, Realization is impossible. Even while doing our various activities throughout the day, japa must go on. Because of constant good thoughts, purification of the blood, mind, intellect, power of memory and general health will take place. By the same token, evil thoughts will destroy the same.

"At present we are very dim, like night lights, but through sadhana we can become bright, spiritually bright. Simply drawing a picture of a bulb will not give us light. Simply saying "I am the Atman" is not the same as a direct experience of it. Effort is needed. The coolness of the breeze, the beams of the moon, the vastness of space—all of these are permeated by God. Knowing and experiencing this Truth is the goal of human birth. Strive for that."

Amma proceeded to Seattle and then returned to the Bay Area, and subsequently spent a few days in Mt. Shasta. When, on the way north, the mountain became visible from the car, Amma began to stare at it intently. She did not know that this mountain, covered at the time with a unique mushroom-shaped cloud, was Mt. Shasta. Amma kept looking at it and finally asked us if that was Mt. Shasta, to which we replied that it was. She continued to gaze at it until we reached our retreat site on the slopes of the hill. The scenery was captivating with the snow-covered mountain behind, the grassy slopes below and dormant volcanic peaks around us. There was no electricity where we stayed, yet we did not feel the inconvenience, being happy in the natural surroundings. After Amma settled down in her room, she asked the local organizers whether there was some kind of regular worship of the mountain being done. They said that as far as they knew, the Native American Indians used to worship the mountain, but at present people only looked upon it as a holy place and an abode of divine beings. Amma then said, "While on the way here, I was attracted by the sight of the cloud over the mountain. Somehow I could not take my eyes away from it. I then saw a living presence within the cloud resembling Lord Shiva with three lines of sacred ash on his forehead. I thought that perhaps this mountain has been worshipped since ancient times as a form of God."

Sitting on the grassy slopes with Amma heightened the mystical effect of the atmosphere, which put everyone in a state of blissful peace. On the final day in this pastoral setting, we wanted to take Amma up the mountain to see the snow, as she had never seen snow in India, but Amma kept insisting on giving darshan until the last moment, and then there was no more time to do anything but return to Oakland. It is my experience that whenever we try to make Amma happy in a mundane way, she will somehow or other frustrate our plans and avail the time for purely spiritual purposes. For one established in the Bliss of God-Realization, what could make her happy? After all, the little happiness that we get from sense objects is nothing but an infinitesimal reflection of the Bliss of God. The moon may appear beautiful at night, and an ignorant child will think that it shines by its own light. Until the sun of Self-Realization rises, the moon of the mind will seem to shine of its own accord, and the bliss that the mind experiences will seem to have an independent existence. Amma was thereby trying to teach us not to seek happiness outside our Real Self. If sages do not set an example for the ignorant, then who will?

From Mt. Shasta we continued on to Santa Fe and Taos. In each place, the schedule was the same as in the Bay Area, and Devi Bhava was held in houses of the hosts of each city. This would not be possible in the coming years, however, because of the increasing crowds, and eventually only large halls would be used for this purpose. On the night of her arrival in Santa Fe, Amma could not get even a wink of sleep. She told us in the morning that the entire night was spent in giving darshan to some funny looking subtle beings who were living in the neighbourhood. When asked what they looked like, Amma replied that they had the torso of an animal and the legs of a human being. She said she had never seen such beings before. By some strange coincidence, in one of the rooms of the house where we were staying, there were a number of figurines that answered exactly to Amma's description. When asked what they were, the owner of the house said they were the images of the gods, *kachinas*, that are worshipped by the local tribes of the Native American Indians. From this, we understood that such beings do exist and can be seen by those who have the eyes to see. Apparently, they recognized who Amma was and flocked to her for her blessings.

One day, during morning satsang, an interesting conversation took place between Amma and a sincere seeker. All seekers find that at some point in their sadhana, their mind is distracted by sexual desires from the goal of God or Self-Realization. One person asked Amma for her guidance in this matter, saying, "Amma, what should one do about lust?"

Amma replied, "Child, there is a natural attraction between males and females which exists in all beings. That subtle attraction will be there until one has realized the Truth, even though one has renounced all worldly pleasures and enjoyments. One may find a sixteen-year-old's lust in a hundred-year-old man. Having inherited this vasana from previous births, it is difficult to overcome. Even this body of ours is a product of the lust of our parents. You were conceived as a result of their intense desire to satiate their lust. Therefore, until Liberation, lust will continue to exist as an obstacle.

"But do not be afraid. Constantly take refuge at the feet of God. Sincerely and wholeheartedly pray to the Beloved, 'Where are You? Please don't allow my mind to waste its time in such thoughts. Let the same energy that is being wasted like this be used for the good of the world. O Beloved, please come and save me.' If we go on praying in this way, we will progress by and by."

The man asked, "Amma, if controlling our sexual tendencies is so difficult, what is the hope for us who are so immersed in the world?"

"Child, when the strong desire for God-Realization takes root in your heart," Amma said, "there will be no room left for worldly desires. When a girl gets a handsome and affectionate boyfriend, her mind cannot think of any other man. In the same way, if your mind is filled with God, it will not dwell on any other thing. When you have a fever, sweet things will taste bitter. Similarly, when you are burning with the longing for God, the taste for the world will go.

"Do not think, 'How is it possible to reach that state? I can never attain Liberation.' Through our prayers and sadhana, we can slowly reach the goal. Always remember that the transitory happiness of sex is wrapped in sorrow. If a hose has a hole in it, the water pressure will decrease. If a pot has a leak, the water will go out, however much you may pour into it. Similarly, the energy that is developed through sadhana will not be seen in those who indulge in excessive sex. When heated, water becomes powerful enough to drive a steam engine. In the same way, through self-control the mind is purified and becomes powerful enough to realize God.

"Child, through cultivation of good character, good thoughts and through the company of saints and sages we can remove three quarters of our negative tendencies; yet it is only after the attainment of Realization that all negative tendencies will be destroyed. Therefore, without being afraid, dejected or in a brooding mood, proceed towards the goal."

Going Abroad

From Santa Fe we went to Madison, Chicago, and then on to Boston, where there were well-attended programs at the Cambridge Zen Center, the Theosophical Society and the Harvard Divinity School. Then, after completing the days that were scheduled in New York, Amma went to hold programs at a retreat site in Rhode Island for a few days. While we were staying there, Ron, a cousin of mine, came to visit Amma. He was a prosperous businessman and at the same time a serious spiritual aspirant. He asked Amma her advice regarding his future. She advised him to continue his work in the world as a service to his employees and to try to observe celibacy. This made a lot of sense to him and he was very happy to hear Amma's words. A few days later we left for Europe.

The atmosphere in Europe was distinctly different from that in America. A sense of old world tradition pervaded everywhere. This was a pleasant change from modern America; yet it did involve some inconvenience. Due to the lack of shopping malls, a lot of extra time was spent searching for even the simplest necessities. Furthermore, we always had to rely on translators since English was the only language we knew. The European devotees were also a bit more reserved than those in America, though in future years the number of people coming to see Amma was to become far greater than in America. Two of the most memorable places that Amma visited were a retreat site in a remote village in Austria and an ashram in the Swiss Alps. Even though the weather was extremely cold, sometimes in the lower thirties Fahrenheit, Amma frequently sat outside, wearing only a cotton sari, and gazed at the picturesque green hills while singing to the Divine Amma the song *Srishtiyum Niye*...

> Creation and Creator art Thou
> Thou art Energy and Truth,
> O Goddess... O Goddess...O Goddess...
>
> Creator of the Cosmos art Thou,
> And Thou art the beginning and the end.
>
> The Essence of the individual soul art Thou,
> And Thou art the five elements as well.

During the Devi Bhava in Austria, I was upset to find a man and woman lying down together in the hall just thirty or forty feet in front of Amma. Throughout the tour, there were similar instances. It was not uncommon to see people hugging, kissing, or massaging each other. Often people were dressed far from modestly, and they laughed or talked very loudly in Amma's presence. All of these things created an irreverent and overly casual atmosphere. Because I was used to the spiritually-cultured ways of the Orient (where most people know how to behave in temples or in the presence of a Mahatma), this upset me. However, Amma forbade me from saying anything to anyone. She was, after all, a newcomer in their midst; and neither was it their fault, for how could people be blamed for not knowing what is appropriate behaviour in a situation they have never experienced before? Still, upon seeing this couple lying on the floor, I asked one of the devotees to request that they get up and show a little more respect for Amma's holy presence. The devotee went over to the couple and sitting down next to them, began by asking a question, "May I ask you something? If the Queen of England was sitting up there on the stage, would the two of you be lying here like this?" The couple was visibly surprised to hear that and said, "Of course not." "Then how can you lie here in front of the Holy Mother? She is the Queen of the Universe." Needless to say, they immediately got up.

Amma spent about ten days in the Swiss Alps in a beautiful ashram setting, surrounded by snow-peaked mountains with magnificent views of emerald green lakes nestled in the valleys below the ashram. Huge crowds of devotees from all over Europe came during the retreat, and it was a memorable occasion for all. During one of the morning darshans, someone asked Amma, "Amma, how can I help the world? Is doing my own sadhana in any way beneficial to the world?"

Amma replied, "Any sadhana that you do will benefit the entire world. The vibrations from chanting your mantra and meditation will purify your own mind as well as the atmosphere around you. Unknowingly, you will spread peace and quietude to those with whom you come into contact. If you are concerned about the welfare of the world, then do your sadhana sincerely. Become like the lighthouse that guides the ships. Shine the light of God in the world.

"Sometimes people come to Amma saying, 'See, there was such-and-such a government scandal; there was this much stock crash.' Children, nothing in this world is eternal. When we are attached to external objects, the result will only be sorrow. It is sorrow which will lead us to God. The Cosmic Consciousness which we call God pervades all creation. But an intellectual understanding of this will not give us peace of mind; we must gain that through experience. To merge in Pure Awareness—that is the thing that is needed.

"There is no short cut to God; sadhana must be performed regularly and with devotion. It is our own effort which will enable us to experience the grace of God which is being showered on us all the time. Therefore, whatever spare time you get, use it to seek God. If you create peace in your own heart by doing sadhana, then that will have a positive effect on your family, your work and so on. That peace and love of God will overflow out of your heart and encourage others to move on the right path.

"You need not preach to people. Lead your life by the standard of Truth, and many people will benefit. Through your sadhana, you will cultivate the eternal virtues in your character. Our practice should develop patience, forbearance, broad-mindedness, compassion, and other virtues in us. Otherwise, there is no benefit. If we sit for one hour of meditation and then get angry five minutes later, all the benefit of the meditation will be lost. People will benefit by one who is living in accordance to Truth, not by one who is merely preaching Truth.

"Amma does not say much because many of you read a lot of books and hear a lot of lectures about spirituality. Now you must gain experience. Make Truth your very own. This is the thing that is to be done."

From Switzerland, we all flew to a tiny island in the Arabian Sea called Male. We thought that after the exertion of the three month tour, Amma may need a day of rest before getting back to the hectic life in India. We had heard that Male was a paradisical place, and it was indeed so. But one first had to go through hell to get to that paradise, for the immigration and customs officials insisted upon taking apart every single suitcase that we had, which meant two or three hours sitting in the airport hassling and haggling. What a sudden shock after the trouble-free formalities of Western countries. It was like being thrown from a refrigerator into a fire. After finally getting out of the airport, we went to the boat jetty and took a ferry to one of the islands, which was about one hour's distance from the main island. It could not have been more than one square acre on which a few rooms had been constructed. The whole thing reminded one of a scene from a South Pacific adventure movie. Apart from the hotel staff, we were the only people there. It was indeed a little paradise, with its white sands and crystal clear lagoons and brilliant red, blue, green and yellow fish swimming all around. That night, Amma sat with all of us under a star-studded sky illumined by a full moon, singing some new songs that were composed during the tour. It was really the closest thing to heaven on earth.

The next morning, when we got into the boat and started back to the main island, the sea soon became very rough, and many of us began to imagine that we would all soon sink into the deep abyss. We eventually reached the island and were "thrilled" to find that the customs officials wanted to open all our suitcases one more time before saying good-bye. We were quite relieved to leave that hellish paradise and very happy when we reached India an hour and a half later. There was a huge crowd to receive Amma in Trivandrum. She was led to an auditorium in the city and given an official reception there. She then made the three hour journey back to Vallickavu in the ashram bus along with all the residents who had been pining to see her for so many days. Even the local villagers, generally ill-disposed towards Amma since the early days of her sadhana, were glad to see her and held a reception in a very grand manner. Not letting the excitement stand in her way, Amma, upon her return, immediately walked around the entire ashram, examining whatever changes had taken place, herself cleaning up any untidy areas. Everyone was overjoyed to have her back. They seemed like dead bodies brought back to life!

Later that year, accepting the invitation of her devotees in Reunion Island and Mauritius, two small islands off the eastern coast of Africa, Amma and a group of brahmacharis left for that destination on December 17, 1987. A disciple of Amma's named Prematma Chaitanya (now Swami Premananda Puri) had built a beautiful little ashram for Amma on Reunion Island, where a huge crowd received her, many of them weeping out of joy at the sight of her. More than a thousand people of all religions attended each of Amma's programs which were held in various parts of the island. These were moments of wonderful religious harmony. It was perhaps the first occasion in the history of Reunion Island's mosque where a non-Muslim spiritual leader was invited and welcomed by the Sufi master of the place. This Sufi had a mystical experience when he once visited Amma's Reunion ashram. As he stood before the beautiful picture of Amma in the meditation hall, he had a vision of Amma stepping out of the picture and standing before him in flesh and blood, to whom he immediately prostrated. Coming out of the hall, he told Prematma, "Today I have seen a Real Mother." He later expressed to the congregation at the mosque, "It is extremely rare to come across a Self-Realized soul, and even if one does, to recognize such a one is even more difficult, for they do not easily reveal themselves. A saint like the prophet Mohammed is soon to visit our island. If you all agree, we can receive her at the airport and invite her to visit the mosque." Everyone gladly agreed, and so that reception took place. Amma gave darshan to everyone there, many people bursting into tears. They were all very sorry to see her leave, for the superficial distinctions of caste and creed had disappeared before her pure love.

From Reunion, Amma went to Mauritius, where she was invited to visit the Governor General at his place of residence. She answered his many questions regarding spirituality and social service. During her three-day stay in Mauritius, she was received at many ashrams and temples on the island, and finally returned to India the first week of January.

Many years ago, when Amma had first started the Krishna Bhava and devotees were still very few, she told her father one Bhava darshan night that she would travel many times around the world and that people from different countries would come to see her in Vallickavu. Of course, he could not believe a word of what she said. Until then, Amma had been like a servant. She had nothing of her own and no future to speak of. Who could have imagined then that an unknown village girl would comfort and console thousands of people from all walks of life? It was that first world tour that bore out the truth of Amma's words. Born out of intuition rather than reason, her knowledge of the future is unfailing. One should not be fooled by her humble appearance. Real sages need not advertise their omniscience. They are understood only when they allow themselves to be so.

CHAPTER 8

Computer Leela

SOON AFTER THE WORLD TOUR, my cousin Ron came to the ashram for a two-week stay. It was a big step for him to come from a life of comfort to the spartan atmosphere of the ashram. But he was more than rewarded through the peace of mind that he felt. One day, I showed him around the ashram library and asked him if it would be possible for him to alphabetize a list of all the books there.

"This job would be very easy for a computer. Don't you have one here?" I found Ron's question very amusing. It was like asking a beggar if he had a Rolls Royce. What would we do with a computer? And where would we have gotten the money to purchase one? I told him that we didn't have a computer nor could I imagine what we would do with one even if we did.

"Well, you could alphabetize your library list by title and author or subject, you could do accounting, office work, or even use it to publish your English books," said Ron. He then offered to purchase a computer for the ashram and requested me to ask Amma if she would agree. I went to Amma and told her about our conversation. She asked me, "What is a computer and what can it do?" I told her what Ron had said.

"If getting us a computer makes him happy, by all means, let him do so, but the money could be better spent on the building construction," Amma replied. I then went and told Ron the first half of the sentence, but I omitted the part about the building construction because I felt that I shouldn't put a damper on his eagerness to give the ashram a computer. Also, after thinking about it for some time, I had grown to like the idea of having a computer at the ashram. Yet when my own enthusiasm led me to abbreviate Amma's words to Ron, little did I know that the purchase of a computer was to mark the beginning of a very painful stage in my life. Until then, I had scrupulously avoided technology feeling it to be a distraction to my spiritual life. Even then, I had no intention of learning to use the computer myself. When I went to Amma again and asked her when we could go to a big city in order to purchase a computer, she was not very happy about the whole thing and told us to go whenever we liked, which was her way of saying, "You're going to do whatever you like anyhow, so why do you ask me?" This is an extremely dangerous situation to get into in relation to Amma, for as I mentioned before, she functions on the level of intuition, not necessarily reasoning. If one implicitly follows her instructions, one's sufferings will be far less than otherwise. But if one knowingly does whatever one likes against her wishes, one can expect endless calamities to follow. If one follows the devotional path of surrender to God's Will, obedience and surrender to the Guru's will is a requirement. But often we forget or disregard the Guru's will since it is our tendency to do what is most pleasing to our own minds. Because of this strong tendency, I was about to learn a bitter but profitable lesson.

The following day, Ron, two other brahmacharis and I went to the big city of Cochin in search of a computer. We finally found one that we liked and placed an order, for there was nothing in stock but a demonstration model. We were told that it would take three weeks for delivery, but until then, they would lend us their own computer. So, back we went to the ashram with our new machine. Now the question was, who was going to learn to use the computer? Because I had a desk, they put the computer in my room. Next, someone went to ask Amma who should learn. She suggested two brahmacharis who had been somewhat familiar with computer science before joining the ashram. But they had very little time for this work and used to come at night for only one or two hours. Now and then they would consult me when they had any difficulty because they thought three heads were better than two. At this point, an insidious idea invaded my mind. "Why not try to learn it a little? Anyhow, it is sitting in my room. If I can learn a little, I can help them also." So went my thoughts.

There is a story about how the mere proximity of a thing spoiled the sadhana of a yogi. There was once a sage who was so intense in his austerities that Indra, the lord of the gods, became afraid that he might some day take his throne in heaven away from him. Indra thought, "I must find some way to foil the penance of this saint and prevent him from rising to the heavenly worlds."

Indra soon conceived of an idea. Disguising himself as a hunter, he went down to earth with a bow and arrows and approached the ashram of the sage. Bowing low to the saint, he said, "O sadhu, I am a hunter and must now make a long journey on foot. I would be most grateful if you would keep this heavy bow and arrows here until I return, as it will be an unnecessary burden for me to carry them."

"A bow and arrows?" exclaimed the saint. "I am sorry, sir, but it would cause me great pain even to see such things here, since they are used to kill animals."

"Swami, I will keep them at the back of your house and you will never see them. Then there will be no disturbance to you and I will be relieved of a great deal of trouble. Can't you help me in this way?"

Compassionate as sadhus are, the saint gave in to the hunter's request and the bow and arrows were left at the back of the sage's hut. The hunter then took his leave and went away.

As it happened, the yogi used to walk around outside his house after his meditation, and thus, he would see the bow and arrows every day. Finally, one day he thought, "Let me just see how this bow and arrow work. Surely no harm will come of it." He picked up the bow and fit an arrow to it. He was surprised at how fast and far the arrow flew. Thereafter, he could not resist the temptation to practice with the bow and arrow a little more each day. Finally, he enjoyed it so much that he became a hunter. Thus, the object that at first he did not even want to see became a source of great pleasure to him and, of course, a huge impediment to his spiritual progress.

With nobody to teach me and no books to study from, I started to learn from scratch, by means of trial and error. As anyone who has used a computer knows, if something goes wrong, it could be any one of a million things, and a lot of things did go wrong. Seeing my interest in learning how to use the computer, the other two brahmacharis stopped coming. I asked them why they weren't coming anymore, and they answered that they had no time. In any case, now the problem arose: a lot of money had been spent on the computer, with me as one of the instigators, and nobody wanted to learn how to use it. Who was going to be blamed for this unnecessary purchase? I could just imagine Amma saying, "Didn't I warn you? You always learn the hard way." I therefore got panicky and decided that, do-or-die, at least one person in the ashram was going to master the computer, and that person ended up being myself. Yet this was easier said than done. I spent many sleepless nights wrestling with that diabolical machine. On countless occasions I was even on the verge of tears, so frustrating was this trial, but through intense prayer and persistence, I did finally attain a moderate proficiency. After that, my work increased tremendously.

Up until that point, I had been engaged in duplicating the ashram's song tapes. All the tape recorders were stacked in my room, one on top of the other, and I would go on endlessly recording day and night, for the demand for the tapes was always greater than the supply. Originally, the ashram would not sell photos of Amma or recordings of her singing. Whenever a devotee would offer to duplicate some photos or tapes, we would accept and then freely distribute the items to whomever asked. But when the requests became too frequent and too many, we had no choice but to sell the tapes and photos at a minimal cost, in order to keep the devotees supplied. As the years went by and the devotees coming to the ashram increased more and more, the demand for tapes also increased. As I could not do any hard physical work due to my troublesome back, the job of copying the tapes fell on me. It was a day and night round-the-clock routine. At night, I would put the tapes in, turn on the machines, lie down, doze off, and when I heard the click of the tape recorders, would get up, turn over the tapes, and again go back to sleep for half an hour until the next click. This went on for a number of years.

My other job was to pump water up to the overhead tank at night. It was only at night that the water came from the municipal supply lines. Because the water pressure was extremely low, we built a tank below ground level in order to get the maximum quantity through gravity feed.

Usually the pressure was so low that it hardly pushed the water one foot above ground level; therefore, I had to pump the water out regularly into the overhead tank so that the incoming tank would again fill up. Doing this job meant, in addition to getting up every half hour for the tapes, I had to stay up for a whole hour every two hours to pump the water. Now the computer work also fell on my shoulders.

Although the computer company had promised to supply our computer within three weeks, the days and weeks went by without our receiving anything. Finally, after six months had passed, the computer slowly began to arrive part by part. The whole computer was there at last, but this was not the end of our troubles. Just as they had arrived week by week, the parts proceeded to break down at the same rate, until every single part had to be replaced. Once everything was working again, the cycle would repeat itself again as the computer continued to break down part by part. The company told me that they had never had an experience like this before. They had an excellent record of performance, they said, and they couldn't understand what was going on at our ashram that was causing such a headache to them and us both. I hesitated to tell them what I knew to be the truth—

that Amma's blessings were not on this computer. I even thought sometimes that perhaps she had actually cursed the whole undertaking.

One day when one of the computer technicians came to do some repair work, he expressed a wish to have Amma's darshan. After bowing down to Amma, he got up and she said to him, "Nealu feels that I have cursed the computer. But I never curse anybody or anything. Why should I? They do a very good job of cursing themselves." After that, the intensity of our computer problems decreased but never completely stopped.

Once our computer was in reasonable working order, it was in such demand that the need for a second computer arose. I hesitatingly went to Amma, explaining that it was not due to some personal idea of mine, but rather that all the ashram work could no longer be done on just one machine. She agreed for me to go to Cochin and purchase another computer. The next morning, when I went to her room to tell her that I was going, she asked me, "Where?" I reminded her that she had agreed for me to go to Cochin for the purchase of a computer, but she claimed to not remember anything about it. Over the next six months, this scene repeated itself four times until finally I decided that I was not going to raise the subject any more. After all, I had come to the ashram to realize God, not to spend time worrying over this troublesome machine. I decided at this point I would have nothing more to do with the computer, a decision which would be made and unmade a thousand times in the future. It gradually became clear to me that Amma had decided that I was going to become the first person in history to realize God in front of a computer! In ancient days, spiritual aspirants used to sit in caves and meditate until their egos became so attenuated that the Light of God could shine through. Perhaps in the present age, monks will attain the same purity of mind by struggling in front of a keyboard and monitor.

The Guru gives us many chances to improve our "track record" of surrender and obedience. It was not much later that I got mine. One day, I found a tiny boil on one of my fingers. After I scratched it a little, it became infected. The wound grew bigger and bigger until half the finger was oozing and burning. I tried treating it with various kinds of ointments and antibiotics, but to no avail. At last, after ten days of suffering, I decided that perhaps I should show it to Amma and ask her advice since medical science was failing to help me. At the same time, I hesitated a bit to ask Amma such a mundane question, so I came up with an idea. I wrapped a piece of cloth around my finger, making a bandage which was as big as a tennis ball and went into her room and sat down after bowing to her. She naturally noticed my hand and asked, as I had hoped she would, what was the matter. I ceremoniously unveiled it. She took one look at it and said, "Oh, why don't you put some turmeric powder on it?" "Turmeric powder," I thought, "what could turmeric powder do that the nuclear bombs of modern medicine couldn't do?"

But the next moment, I remembered that Amma's words should not be taken lightly, and so I left the room and went straight to the ashram kitchen. After searching around for some time, I finally came across a plastic bag of turmeric powder which had obviously been used for cooking. At first I thought, "People might have put their grimy hands in here and it is not clean enough to put on the wound." But then I realized that Amma's will does not depend on cleanliness for its fruition. Rubbing some of the turmeric on the wound, I felt immediate relief from the burning sensation and within a week it completely healed. Seeing this, I thought that I had discovered a new miracle drug. Since I was also assisting in the medical dispensary and dressing wounds, I applied turmeric powder to the next wound I treated and covered it with a bandage. What was my surprise when the patient came back two days later with a beautiful infection, even worse than before. Apparently, it was not the turmeric that had cured me but Amma's omnipotent will.

CHAPTER 9

Brahmasthanam – Abode of the Absolute

NOT LONG AFTER SHE RETURNED from abroad, Amma decided to construct and consecrate a unique kind of temple in a village called Kodungaloor, about four hours north of the ashram. This temple is called Brahmasthanam (Abode of the Absolute), and it has four doors opening out to the four cardinal points. The installed image is a composite one, sculpted from a single stone, containing four different deities, one on each side. They are Lord Shiva, Devi, Lord Ganesha (the Remover of obstacles), and Rahu, who in the form of a snake, represents one of the "planets" that influence human destiny. (In Western astrology, Rahu is the north node of the moon.) The Brahmasthanam, as conceived by Amma, serves as an unfailing refuge for the many who are caught in the whirlpool of malefic planetary influences. The idea of such a temple occurred to Amma while examining the cause of the suffering of the millions who have come to her in search of relief for their many inexplicable ills. Amma feels that the positions and movements of the planets and other heavenly bodies have a direct or indirect impact on human lives. The malefic influences are generally caused by the position and movements of the planets Saturn, Mars and the shadowy Rahu. She decided there must be some effective means to overcome the evil influences. Therefore, she inaugurated a puja in this temple to nullify the ill effects of these planets and their periods of transition.

Actual participation in performing the puja at the Brahmasthanam temple ensures quick, positive results for the afflicted. If done earnestly and in the right spirit, no act of worship can go without its result. The pujas performed at Amma's Brahmasthanam temples, since their first inception at Kondungaloor, have been known to result in the purification of the atmosphere. A second temple was established at Amma's ashram in Madras, and in May 1990, the seven-day ritual, in which over a thousand people participated, resulted in the much-needed rain to relieve the drought in the Madras area. For the purification of the mind and for the expansion of spiritual qualities in one's life, it is not enough to simply go to a temple or church and pay one's obeisance and return home. It is necessary to do some form of spiritual practice and establish the Lord in one's heart through devotion that is based on spiritual principles. It is to lead people to that goal that Amma has developed the Brahmasthanam temple and its mode of worship.

In ancient times, it was the Great Masters who did the installation of images. Amma says, "The installation of sacred images should not be performed by those who are unable to keep their own life force steady. It must be done by those who are able to infuse *prana shakti* (life force) into the image and thereby instill a living presence (*chaitanya*) into it. Only if done by such sages will the chaitanya in the image grow and increase when the puja is regularly performed."

If one were to study the history of ancient temples, one would find perfect veracity in Amma's statements. Famous temples like Tirupati Venkateswara and Guruvayoor Krishna are examples of temples consecrated by ancient sages. They attract millions of devotees every year. The images installed by them, though outwardly appearing like a stone, are actually reflections of the effulgence of the Supreme Being. Such images are filled with divine power and can grant the boons sought after by devotees. There are many such images in India.

Some people may question why temples and images of deities are necessary since the goal of Self-Realization is to experience the Absolute in which no duality exists. About this Amma says, "Those who have reached the state of Non-Dual Realization may say that none are born nor do they die, for they have no body-consciousness. Indeed, *they* are not born nor do they die. However, have all people reached this state of Non-Duality? Don't most other people have body-consciousness? For the most part, their minds are weak, being absorbed only in worldliness. They do not have the knowledge of their innate Perfection, and therefore they are affected by worldly activities and come to grief. If you advise such people in an *Advaitic* (non-dual) way, it is difficult for them to suddenly relate to that in their daily life and to move forward. We may advise them, 'You are not the body,' but those who live their lives in the world know its difficulties. So even if you tell them, 'You are not the body, mind or intellect,' it is not their experience. Although they may know it to be a fact, they are immersed in the world and cannot suddenly transform themselves and experience it in their daily lives. Advaita is the Truth, but that advice should not be given abruptly. It is not correct to tell a child who is crying due to an injured hand, 'Don't cry. It is only the body and you are not the body.' The child will still continue to cry from the pain. Such is the state of those who live in the world. They are affected by planetary conjunctions and will have to undergo suffering in accordance with their fructifying evil karmas.

"Amma has seen at least ten million people. Even those who own ships and airplanes have stories of sorrow and come as devotees in search of peace. Amma knows all about the suffering which they undergo during the malevolent conjunctions of the planets. These temples have been constructed in order to give relief to such persons.

"Nowadays, how many people are there in the country who have faith in God? Real devotion to temples is not to be found. Many even try to destroy the temples! Nevertheless, if the principles involved in temple worship are convincingly explained to them, a transformation can be brought about. When the approach is through reasoning, it is possible to inculcate devotion in such people as well. It is for this reason that Amma has built these temples.

"The nature of the image installed at Kodungaloor is 'unity in diversity and diversity in unity.' Don't diverse materials become one as ash, when offered into the fire and burnt? Similarly, in the Fire of Knowledge, multiplicity gets reduced to Unity. Oneness has to be seen in the various faces. The Divine Power residing in all is only one. When we look at a person having eyes, nose, arms and legs, we do not see him as those varied organs but as a single human form composed of all these. Similarly, though each body is a separate unit, one should see the identity of the One Self which propels all. That is the concept here.

"Pressing a single switch, we can have any number of bulbs illumined. Here in the Brahmasthanam, four 'lights' have been connected to one 'switch,' that's all. Through a single resolve of Amma's, the life energy has been infused into the four deities. What is called 'energy' is only one. Why should the four be installed in four different places? Thus, all four have been placed in a single stone. Also, one should consider that to install these deities in separate places would require that much more space. Isn't the concept more important than the question of how or where the installation is done?

"Children, God is not in the stone. Isn't He in our own hearts? It is to remove the dirt from one's face that one looks into a mirror. We ourselves are not in the mirror. God is everywhere, but in order to purify the human mind and remove the dirt there from, a medium is needed. We should develop a conception in our mind. The sacred image is for that purpose. Some people worship a mountain as God. What is important is each one's conception or attitude. Similarly, this temple and image installed therein is Amma's conception. It is predominantly Shiva-Shakti. In ancient times there were no temples. One's heart alone was the temple. How long ago have temples come into existence? Not very long ago. In order to lead people forward in accordance with their nature, the Mahatmas installed different divine forms in different ages.

"The nature of Lord Shiva is the State of the Absolute. Only the Absolute (Brahman) has the capacity to remove all impurities. Lord Shiva alone takes up and swallows, by Himself, the evil consequences of the wicked actions of all beings. Lord Shiva is the filter that receives the evil karmas of both humans and gods. The Lord's nature is to receive the impurities of humanity and thereby purify them. He is unaffected, no matter how much impurity He absorbs and He Himself can save the world. Lord Ganesha is the one who removes obstacles or impediments. Removing the obstructions, Devi, the Divine Energy, (*kundalini shakti*), dormant in the base of the spine (*muladhara chakra*), is awakened and emerges in the shape of a serpent, moving upward until it reaches Shiva (the Formless State of the Absolute). This is the principle implied in the Brahmasthanam. Amma's aim is not merely to bind people to the worship of the image; she wishes for their Realization."

CHAPTER 10

Tests of Faith

AMMA'S SECOND WORLD TOUR started in May of 1988. Having experienced or heard about Amma's Divine Love the previous year, many more people came to see her. In each place, the halls were full to overflowing. In Singapore, one lady bowed down to Amma and when she got up, Amma asked her, "Why didn't you come back the next day?" The lady had a shocked expression on her face and then was overjoyed. She later related to us that the previous year when she had come to see Amma, Amma had asked her to come back the next day, but because of unavoidable circumstances, she could not. This was the meaning of Amma's question. The lady was shocked that Amma, who must have seen hundreds of thousands of people since, could have remembered such an insignificant incident. This convinced her of Amma's divinity.

It would not be out of place here to mention something about siddhis or mystic powers. Many miracles take place around Amma. She also displays a definite and unfailing omniscience. Even though she pretends not to know something, it seems obvious to her devotees that this is only a pretence. How many thousands of people have experienced her omniscience! And how many thousands more have experienced her saving grace pulling them out of their insolvable problems! Amma does not flaunt her powers. She is much too subtle for that. Yet she does not deny that Mahatmas can and do perform what seem to be to us, miraculous things. When questioned about the nature of miracles and spiritual powers, she replied:

"Miracles are usually attributed to god men. There is a general concept that miracles can only be performed by a divine being, that miracles are part and parcel of such a person. People even believe that if a person doesn't perform any miracles, he or she cannot be a great soul, even though he may, in fact, be Self-Realized. But the truth is that our idea of what constitutes a miracle may or may not happen in the presence of the truly great ones, because they really don't care that much about it. They have nothing to gain or lose by performing miracles. They don't care about name or fame, nor do they wish to please or displease anyone. If it happens, that's fine, and if it doesn't happen, that too is fine. In the modern age, however, people's faith in God depends on the miracles a Self-Realized master or a god man performs. There are, unfortunately, also so-called gurus who exploit people by appearing to perform miracles.

"To have absolute mastery over the mind is the same as having mastery over the universe. Everything in creation is made of the five elements: fire, water, earth, air, and space. Once you attain God-Realization, all these five elements are under your control; they become your obedient servants. If you want something to turn into a mountain, it will do so; or if you wish to create another world, that is also possible. But for this to happen, you don't actually have to reach the final point of Realization. You could gain this ability even before that.

"A person may possess miraculous powers, but as long as he is in the grip of the ego and the feeling of 'I' and 'mine,' those powers are useless, because his basic nature remains unchanged, and he himself cannot change or transform anyone. Such a person cannot lead anyone on the path to divinity. A person who misuses his powers can only destroy and do harm to society. By using his powers against the laws of nature, he is inevitably paving the way for his own destruction.

"In fact, by performing miracles, one is upsetting the laws of nature. Of course, a Self-Realized soul is free to do so, because he is one with the cosmic energy, but he does it only if it is absolutely necessary. He would prefer to refrain from it as much as possible.

"The government, with the help of administrative experts, makes the constitution of a country, and they themselves have to abide by the rules and regulations they have created. Similarly, the true masters are the ones who have set the laws of nature, but in order to set an example, they themselves have to abide by the rules without going beyond and disrupting them.

"Spirituality is not meant to feed the ego. Spirituality gets rid of the ego; it teaches one to go beyond the ego. Anyone can develop occult powers by performing certain practices as prescribed by the scriptures. But true spiritual realization is something far beyond such things. It is the state in which you become completely free from all bondage, from the bondage of body, mind, and intellect. It is the inner experience of the Supreme Truth. Once that final point has been reached, one cannot harbour any negative feelings such as anger, hatred, or vengefulness. In that state, you dwell in supreme peace and divine love, irrespective of time or place; and wherever you are, you radiate that same peace and love. The divine love, compassion, and peace which you radiate will transform the minds of people. Such a being can change mortals into immortals, the ignorant into wise ones, and man into God. That is the true miracle, which happens in the presence of a Mahatma.

"In a Mahatma's presence, miracles may happen spontaneously; it is simply an integral expression of his existence. By a mere glance of the master, or by his wish, everything is transformed into whatever he wants. But one must have the proper attitude and the right insight to perceive the real miracles that are happening around the Master.

"A person who has become one with the Supreme Consciousness is also one with all of Creation. He is no longer just the body. He is the one life force which shines in everything in Creation. He is the Consciousness that lends its beauty and vitality to everything. He is the Self that is immanent everywhere.

"There is a story about the great sage, Vedavyasa, and his son, Suka. Even as a boy, Suka was detached from the world. Vedavyasa wanted his son to get married and to lead the normal life of a householder. But Suka, who was born divine, was strongly inclined to live the life of a renunciate. So, one day he gave up everything and left to become a sannyasi. While Suka was walking away, Vedavyasa called his son's name. It was Nature that responded to his call—the trees, the plants, the mountains, valleys, birds, and animals—they all answered him. But what exactly does this mean?

"When Vedavyasa called his son, Nature answered, because Suka was that Pure Consciousness which is immanent in all of Nature. Vedavyasa called Suka, but Suka was not the body and therefore had no name or form. He was beyond name and form. He existed within everyone; the bodies of all creatures were his. He was in every body, and therefore everything responded. This is the meaning of the story.

"To go beyond the ego means that one becomes one with the universe. You become as expansive as the universe. You dive deep into its secret mysteries and realize the ultimate reality, the Supreme Truth. You become the master of the universe.

"Amma never felt separated in any way from her true Self. So it is difficult to say at what point this miraculous power started working. There was never a moment when Amma did not experience her oneness with the Supreme Power. From birth itself, Amma knew that there was nothing but God alone."

During the second world tour, in addition to the countries she visited the previous year, Amma also went to England and Germany. One day in Munich during

Amma's daytime darshan, I went for a long walk. Unexpectedly, I came upon an old palace that had been converted into a museum. In front of the palace was a pond containing a number of large white swans and huge fish. I thought that Amma might like to see them and informed her of it after the darshan. She became like a little child in her eagerness to see the swans, for in the Indian scriptures, it is told that there are swans in the Manasarovar Lake in Tibet near the famous Mt. Kailash, which is the legendary abode of Lord Shiva. According to the scriptures, swans have the unique ability of separating milk from water. They are able to do so because of the acid secretion in their mouth that causes the milk to curdle, leaving the water behind. They are symbolic of the quality of discrimination between the real and the unreal. What is real and what is unreal? That which never changes, which is the same in the past, present and future is real, and all else is unreal. This is the definition that the ancient sages gave for Reality. Everything in creation is a mixture of both. Forms are unreal, but their essence is real, and that pervades everything like milk in water. If one discriminates within oneself as to what is it that never changes, one will find the Truth.

We went to the pond on the way to the evening program, and Amma went running over to the swans. She

Tests of Faith

fed them pieces of bread which they ate out of her hands, and she giggled and laughed like a little girl.

Amma spent ten days in the Swiss Alps, a couple of hours drive from Zurich. During her stay there, she spoke to a devotee who was obsessed with the fear of death. "God has given you a proper aura. It has unlimited, infinite energy. It can be charged to any extent. We can travel in any world, even in a world devoid of air. Death can be transcended. You are never born; you never die. If the fan or refrigerator or light bulb breaks, the electric current is not destroyed. In a like manner, the Atman in you is ever-existing. Do not fear death, and do not worry about the next birth."

Another person asked, "Amma, every day I devote some time to meditation, but the desired benefit is not obtained."

Amma replied, "Son, your mind is entangled in so many matters. Regularity and discipline in life are of great necessity for a spiritual aspirant. If you do sadhana without these, how can you derive any benefit? If you take some oil in a vessel and then transfer it to another vessel and another vessel and so on, finally there will be nothing left. Where did it go? It got stuck to the sides of all the vessels. In a similar manner, if you involve yourself in many worldly affairs, after doing meditation, the power that is gained from concentration on a single object will be lost in the maze of diversity. If you can see the oneness of God in the diverse objects of the world, then you will not lose the power you gain through meditation."

One day after Amma's arrival back in India, a telegram came from Paris. It was from the French brahmachari who had arranged Amma's European programs. He had lived in the ashram for about six years when the government decided not to extend his visa any longer. When he asked Amma what to do, she told him that he should go to France and teach classes on spirituality. He was, of course, very upset, for he wanted to spend the rest of his life near Amma, as all of the rest of us wanted. At that time, there was no hint of Amma going around the world; at least we had no idea, although Amma knew fully well that she would go to America and Europe. Everyone including Amma saw the brahmachari off at the train station with a tearful farewell. With only a few dollars in his pocket and no friends to speak of in France, he returned to Paris in a dejected mood. Yet he had the faith that as it was Amma's will that he should go, everything would turn out all right. First he stayed in a church and then spent a few days in the houses of some of the people he had come into contact with there, giving talks here and there about Amma and Vedanta, the philosophy of Non-Dualism. Finally, his father, with whom he had little contact even before this, offered him a tiny, unheated room on the top of a building owned by him. He started to travel to different parts of France, England, Austria, Germany, Switzerland, Belgium and Italy, giving classes in each place. He would travel nearly five thousand miles in a month. When Amma's American tour was proposed, the devotees in Europe also expressed their eagerness for her to visit there, and so he made all the arrangements for that. But because of his hectic routine and excessive travels, his health suffered, and finally he developed glaucoma in both eyes. In his telegram to Amma he wrote, "The doctors say that I may lose my sight because of glaucoma. I have no money for treatment. Let Amma's will be done." While reading the telegram, tears came to Amma's eyes, and she got up and moved off to a corner of the ashram to be alone. She sat there in meditation for some time and then called one of the brahmacharis and asked him to go the nearest town where there was a direct-dialing telephone and call the brahmachari in France and tell him not to worry and that money would be sent to him. When he returned about six hours later after making the phone call, he told Amma that the brahmachari had just come back from the doctor and that not one but three doctors had examined his eyes and found no sign of the glaucoma anymore! This was considered as a miracle by them, but the French brahmachari knew the truth, that Amma had intervened.

A real Guru will put a disciple through severe tests of faith after a certain stage has been reached in their relationship. This is not out of cruelty but only to ultimately bless the disciple with a chance to develop perfect faith, to exhaust their past bad karma, and to ultimately liberate them from the cycle of birth and death. Spiritual life is no joke and only those who are ready to die for God-Realization should take to it fully, for the deeper one goes, the more demanding it becomes. There are many stories in the literature of the world of the tests the disciples have been put through by their Gurus.

There is a story about a devotee who was a wealthy landlord who owned a whole village. His form of devotion was to worship the tomb of a holy man. But one day he heard a great Guru during a satsang which made such a profound impression on him that he decided to seek initiation from the Guru.

The Guru was an omniscient being, yet he asked the devotee whom he was following at present, to which he replied the name of the deceased saint. "I will grant you initiation after you have gone back to your house and dismantled your puja room," said the Guru. The devotee ran to his house as fast as he could and tore down every brick of the room. A number of people who had gathered to watch him solemnly warned him, "Brother, you will have to pay very heavily for the desecration of this holy room. We would not like to be in your shoes."

He boldly replied, "I have done it willingly and am ready to suffer any and all consequences." When he returned to the Guru, the Master bestowed initiation on him.

But it was destined that he should be put to still further tests. Soon his horse died, then some of his bullocks. Thieves stole his possessions. Then the people began to taunt him, saying, "This is the result of the disrespect shown to the departed saint. You should go and rebuild the temple in your home." But none of this bothered him. He said, "I do not care what happens. My Guru is all-knowing and he knows what is best. Of that, nothing can shake my belief."

But one misfortune followed another, and before long he was not only destitute, but owed money to many people. All of them demanded immediate repayment saying, "Either pay us or leave the village immediately." Many of his friends pleaded with him saying, "If you would only rebuild the temple, things would be sure to take a turn for the better." But the devotee remained adamant and preferred to leave the village. So he and his wife and daughter packed up their few remaining belongings and found shelter in another village. As he had been a rich landlord, he had never had to learn a trade. But it was now necessary for him to earn some money, so he began to make his livelihood by cutting and selling grass.

Several months went by in this way, when one day the Guru sent him a letter which was delivered by one of his disciples. To the disciple, the Guru said, "Please be sure to demand twenty rupees as an offering before you give him the letter. If he does not pay you, bring back the letter." The devotee was delighted to see the letter, but he had no money to pay the fee. He asked his wife what to do and she said, "I will take my ornaments and those of my daughter and sell them to the goldsmith." The goldsmith offered them exactly twenty rupees which was given to the disciple. The devotee received the letter, kissed it and held it to his heart. At that moment he went into samadhi.

But the Guru wished to test him still further, and so he told one of his disciples, "Ask him to come to my ashram." The devotee and his family ran to the Guru's ashram and settled down there. They went to work in the kitchen cleaning vessels and cutting firewood. After a few days, the Guru asked, "Where does that new devotee eat his food?" "He eats with all the rest of us, getting his food from the free kitchen," replied one of the disciples. "It seems to me," said the Guru, "that he is not doing real service. If he did, he would expect nothing in return for his work. He is charging us for his wages, which he takes in the form of food."

When the devotee heard this from his wife, he said, "I want nothing in return for service to the beloved Guru, who has given me the priceless gem of my mantra. We will get our food by some other means." So from that day on, he went to the forest each night to cut wood and sold it in the bazaar and used the proceeds to buy food. During the daytime, he and his wife continued to work in the kitchen.

Some time later, he had gone to the forest to cut wood when there was a great wind storm. The wind was so fierce that it blew him and his bundle of wood into a well. The Guru was aware of everything and called some of his disciples and told them to get a board and some rope and follow him to the forest.

When they reached the forest, the Guru said, "He is at the bottom of this well. Shout down to him and tell him that we will lower a board tied to a rope. Tell him to cling to the board and we will pull him out." He also added some words privately to one disciple, the one who was to call into the well.

After shouting into the well, the disciple added, "Brother, see the wretched condition you are in. And it is all due to the way the Guru has treated you. Why don't you forget a Guru who does such things?" "What? Forget the beloved Guru? Never!" shouted the devotee. "And as for you, ungrateful one, please never again speak so disrespectfully of the Guru in my presence. It makes me suffer agony to hear such shameful words."

He was then asked to catch hold of the board, but he insisted that the wood be pulled out of the well first. "It is for the Guru's kitchen and I am afraid that it will get wet and not burn," he said. Finally he came out of the well and came face to face with the Satguru who said to him,

"Brother, you have gone through many trials and have met all of them with courage, faith and devotion to the Satguru. Please ask for some gift or boon. You have earned it and it would make me very happy to give it to you."

At this, the devotee fell on his knees before his beloved Master and with tears streaming down his cheeks, he exclaimed, "What boon could I wish for but you alone? Nothing else could ever be of any interest to me."

Upon hearing these words spoken from his heart, the Guru embraced him and said,

"You are the darling of your Guru,
And Guru is your only love.
Now you, like the Guru,
Are a ship that carries people safely across
The ocean of life and death."

Later in the year, my cousin Ron finally decided that he had enough of worldly life and disposed of his business. From the time he had met Amma, he had been leading a celibate life and had been practicing more and more sadhana. The last time that he had seen Amma he was on his way to signing a contract to internationalize his company. When he asked Amma her opinion, she said that if he was really interested in spiritual progress, it would be better if he did not get involved any deeper in business than he already was. His faith in Amma was such that he didn't sign the contract, thus willingly passing by an opportunity any other businessman would have jumped for. He eventually disposed of his business and purchased a beautiful site in the hills southeast of San Francisco which became Amma's American ashram, the Mata Amritanandamayi Center.

It was around this time that a woman from the village of Parippally, which is located about two hours to the south of the ashram, came to see Amma with a proposal to sell her orphanage. Due to straitened circumstances, she could no longer maintain the institution, and the children who were staying there were undergoing a lot of suffering because of that. Amma did not immediately respond to this proposal, for she wanted to thoroughly investigate the situation first. It was found that the orphanage was indeed deeply in debt and would require a great deal of money to pull it out. Buildings were in a state of utter neglect and dilapidation. There were no toilets or bathrooms for the more than four hundred children who were staying there. They were bathing by the side of the well and allowing the dirty water to flow back into the well, which in its turn, was making them sick with dysentery. They were using any open space available for nature calls. Their diet consisted of wheat flour rolled into balls and boiled with a little salt added. Over all, the whole scene was a pitiful one, and for this reason Amma ultimately decided to assume responsibility for it.

During Amma's next world tour, the orphanage was fully renovated with appropriate bathrooms and toilets, and a clean and regular water supply was installed. A nutritious diet was provided for the children, and a sense of cleanliness and discipline was inculcated through the presence of a number of ashramites who resided there, teaching the children basic health, yogic postures, meditation and devotional singing. Part of the orphanage consisted of a neglected Sanskrit high school, which was also acquired and from which students eventually began winning first prize in many of the state competitions. Eventually, extra-curricular activities like sports, music, art and drama would be added, supervised by the brahmacharis and brahmacharinis.

CHAPTER 11

Liberation of a Great Devotee

OTTOOR UNNI NAMBOODIRIPAD was a famous poet and Sanskrit scholar devotee. He was an authority on the Srimad Bhagavatam. Ottoor's poems glorifying Krishna are loved and appreciated by devotees everywhere. He had won many titles and awards for his gifted poetry. He first met Amma in 1983 when he attended her thirtieth birthday celebration after having heard about her from one of her devotees. Ottoor, who was eighty-five at the time, became like a two year old child in his relationship with Amma. He looked upon her as an incarnation of his beloved Deity, Lord Krishna, as also of the Divine Mother. He decided to spend the rest of his life in Amma's presence and began to compose poems on her.

Amma gave Ottoor the pet name, 'Unni Kanna' (baby Krishna) for his childlike attitude towards her. Sometimes

Liberation of a Great Devotee

one could hear him calling loudly from his room, "Amma! Amma!" at the top of his voice whenever he desired to see her. If Amma happened to be near by, she would go to see him. Though he was suffering a lot due to old age, the moments spent with Amma made him forget about his physical travails.

After coming to Amma, Ottoor wrote the following song:

O Amma
You are the embodiment of both
Krishna and Kali.

O Amma
You sanctify the worlds
with Your smile and Your song,
with Your glance, Your touch
and Your dance,
with Your delightful talk,
by the touch of Your Holy Feet,
and by the nectar of Your Love.

O Amma
Who is the celestial creeper
joyously and bounteously
bestowing all the goals of life
from dharma to moksha,
to all sentient and insentient beings
from Lord Brahma down to a blade of grass.

O Amma
Who astonishes the three worlds,
inundating all human beings
and the bees and the birds,
the worms and the trees
by the turbulent waves of Your love.

Ottoor had only one wish. Whenever he received Amma's darshan, his only prayer to her was, "Amma, when I breathe my last, let my head rest on your lap. This is my only wish, my only prayer. O my Amma, please let me die with my head on your lap." Whenever he met Amma, he would repeat this request.

Soon after Ottoor met Amma, he became a permanent resident of the ashram. He would say, "Now I know that God has not abandoned me, because I am living in His presence and I am basking in His divine love. I used to feel greatly disappointed when I thought of the fact that I couldn't be with Lord Krishna or any of the great saints, but I don't feel that way anymore, because I believe that Amma is all of them."

Just before Amma's third world tour in 1989, Ottoor's health took a turn for the worse. He became very weak and his eyesight was failing rapidly. His well-known prayer to be allowed to die in Amma's lap became constant. When his eye sight became very poor, Ottoor said to Amma,

Amma with Otoor

"It's okay if Amma wants to take away my external sight. But, O Divine Amma of the heavens, kindly bless your servant by removing the inner darkness and open the inner eye. Please don't refuse the prayer of this child."

To this, Amma lovingly replied, "Unni Kanna, don't worry! It will definitely happen. How can Amma refuse your innocent prayer?"

Ottoor was not afraid of death. His only fear was that he would die when Amma was abroad. He expressed this fear to Amma and said, "Amma, I know that you are everywhere and that your lap is as big as the universe. Still, I pray for you to be physically present when I leave my body. If I die while you are away, my wish to die in your lap will not be fulfilled."

Amma caressed him affectionately and replied with great authority, "No, my son, Unni Kanna, that will not happen! You can be sure that you will leave your body only after Amma's return." This was a great consolation to Ottoor. As this assurance came directly from Amma's own lips, Ottoor firmly believed that death couldn't touch him before Amma came back.

After Amma's three month tour, she returned to the ashram in August. During her absence, Ottoor had been undergoing treatment in the home of an ayurvedic doctor.

Amma told him to return to the ashram, as the time for him to leave his body was drawing near.

One night after Devi Bhava, Amma went to Ottoor's room. He was very weak but happy to see her. He wept like a child and prayed to Amma, "O Amma, Mother of the Universe, please call me back! Please call me back, quickly!" Amma caressed his head and rubbed his chest and forehead to comfort him.

Someone had given Amma a new mattress which she wanted to be used by Ottoor. After having it brought to his room, Amma picked up Ottoor's frail body from the bed, and like a mother carrying a baby in her arms, held Ottoor in her arms, while the others spread the new mattress on the cot. As Ottoor was experiencing this demonstration of Amma's compassion, he cried out, "O Amma, Mother of the Universe, why are you showering so much love and compassion upon this unworthy child? O Amma, Amma, Amma..."

Amma lay him gently down on the cot and said, "Unni Kanna, my son, sleep well. Amma will come in the morning."

"O Amma, put me to eternal sleep," replied Ottoor.

Amma once again glanced lovingly at Ottoor before she left the room.

That night, the poet dictated one last song:
Treating me and hoping for a cure
the physicians admitted their defeat.
All my relatives have turned despondent.
O Amma, lay me on Your lap
with tender love
Save me and never forsake me.

O Saradamani, O Sudhamani,
O Holy Amma
Lay me fondly in Your tender lap
Reveal the moon of Ambadi on Your face
Tarry not to bless me with immortality.

Reveal Uncle Moon, Nanda's son
on Your sweet face
and lay this little Kanna on Your lap.
O Amma, lull him to sleep.

At seven the next morning, Amma sent for Ottoor's attendant, Narayanan. When he arrived, she told him that Ottoor was going to leave his body in a few hours. Amma further told Narayanan to find out from his uncle whether he wanted his mortal frame to be buried at the ashram or at his birth place. Narayanan went back to the room and conveyed to his uncle what Amma had said. Though his voice was very feeble, Ottoor clearly replied as he gestured emphatically with his hand, "I will be buried here, in this sacred land. There is nowhere else."

At about ten o'clock, Ottoor asked one brahmacharini, who was standing by his side, to call Amma. She left the room, and for the next few minutes one could see Ottoor's lips moving as he constantly chanted, "Amma, Amma, Amma..." During this chanting, Ottoor went into a samadhi-like state.

At this time, Amma was in her room. As the brahmacharini came in through the door, Amma said, "In a few minutes, my son Ottoor is going to leave his body. But it is not yet time for Amma to be there. Now, his mind is completely focused on Amma. This intense thought is now culminating in a state of *layana* (absorption). When this happens, Amma will go to him. The intensity would have been reduced if Amma had gone to him earlier." A few seconds later, Amma left her room and went over to Ottoor's room. Amma entered the room smiling and sat down on the bed close to Ottoor. With a blissful glow on her face, She kept gazing at his face, as if telling him, "Come, my son! My darling Unni Kanna, come and merge in Me, your eternal Mother." As Amma had predicted earlier, in her room, Ottoor was lying in a state of absorption. Even though Ottoor was in a state of samadhi, his eyes remained half open. There was no sign of any pain or struggle on his face. One could easily see how absorbed and blissful he was. Amma slowly moved closer to his head. She gently lifted it and placed it on her lap. And as Amma held her darling son's head in her lap, she held her right hand on his chest, and continued to gaze at his face.

As he lay on her lap, Amma gently caressed his eyelids, and they were closed forever. Ottoor left his body and his soul merged with Amma for all eternity. Amma bent down and placed a loving, affectionate kiss on his forehead.

Ottoor had written the following poem twenty-five years before Amma's birth:

> When will I hear
> the auspicious names of Kanna
> sounding in my ears?
>
> And upon hearing them
> when will my hairs stand on end
> and I will be immersed in tears?
>
> Being immersed in tears
> when will I become pure?
> And in that state of absolute purity

when will I sing His Names
spontaneously?
And as I sing in ecstasy
when will I forget the earth and the sky?
And forgetting everything
when will I dance
in utter devotion?
And as I dance, will my steps
sweep the stains
from the stage of the world?

In that playful dance
in which I sweep all stains away
I will cry out loud
And through that cry,
will my purity be sent
in the eight directions?
And when the play has been enacted
when will I fall at last
into my Amma's lap?
And lying on my Amma's lap
when will I sleep blissfully?

As I sleep
when will I dream
of the beautiful form of Sri Krishna
who dwells within my heart?
And as I wake up
when will I see Sri Krishna
the Enchanter of the world?

Now this composition was fulfilled by the all-compassionate Amma of the Universe.

Amma sat the whole day next to his body while the *Bhagavad Gita* was chanted over and over again. At night the brahmacharis carried his body to the back of the ashram and cremated him, Amma looking on all the while. What grace! May we all have such a blessed end.

CHAPTER 12

The Vows of Renunciation

IN OCTOBER OF THE SAME YEAR, in a solemn atmosphere of devotion and joy, amidst the chanting of Vedic mantras and puja, one of Amma's sons, who was known as Balu when he first came to Amma in 1979 and later became Brahmachari Amritatma Chaitanya, was ceremoniously initiated into *sannyasa*. Amma gave him the name of Swami Amritaswarupananda Puri. Another sannyasi, a devotee of Amma's by the name of Swami Dhruvananda, performed the traditional fire ceremony and other rituals. The rites of initiation began the previous night. Amma was present throughout the ceremony, showering her blessings and giving advice and instruction. The ceremony was complete by the break of dawn the next day.

Speaking to the assembled devotees, Amma said, "Today Amma is happy because she could dedicate a son for the good of the world. It is eleven years since Balu has first come to the ashram after completing his B.A. exams. In those days, there was Krishna Bhava followed by Devi Bhava. One night during Krishna Bhava, Amma heard somebody singing. Suddenly, Amma felt an attraction in her mind. Though she had heard many people singing songs, when she heard his voice, she felt, 'This is a *loka putra* (son for the whole world) alone, this is a loka putra alone.'

"Even though Amma had seen the one who sang in her mind, she was inspired to stretch and look at him with her own eyes. When that son came inside the temple for darshan, Amma asked, 'Son, for what have you come? Is it to know whether you will succeed in the exams? Son, Amma is crazy.' The first thing that son said was, 'Amma give some of that craziness to me also.' Amma will not initiate anyone so easily, but Amma's mind whispered that this son should be given initiation on that day itself.

"From that day onwards, he would come almost every darshan day. His family protested. As his mother had died when he was a child, his father was the main one to protest. His grandmother was the one who loved him the most. Every month she used to give him one hundred rupees. One day, when he went to get the money, his grandmother asked, 'Are you going to see that girl in Vallickavu?' He couldn't stand there due to a mixture of anger and anguish. 'Didn't she call my Amma a girl?' Returning the money, he immediately left the house.

The Vows of Renunciation 249

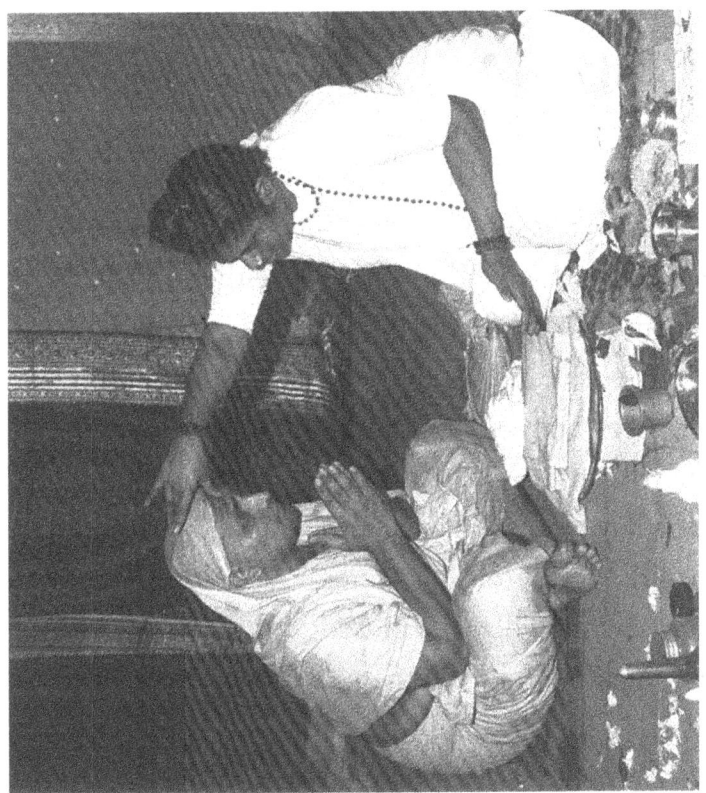

Amma blessing Swami Amritaswarupananda during his initiation into sannyasa

"On the same day when Amma went to a house for puja, she saw him sitting there crying. When Amma asked, 'Son, why are you crying?' he said, 'Grandmother called my Amma a "girl." Hereafter, I don't need her money or her love.' Amma told him, 'Son, Grandma doesn't know anything about Amma. That is why she said that. Therefore, you should still love her and forgive her.'

"After some time, when there was not enough money in the ashram, this son started selling his pants and shirts. His family members did not like this either. In addition to overcoming the difficulties in his house, when that son came to the ashram, he also had to bear the opposition and abuse of Sugunanandan Acchan (Amma's father) and the villagers.

"One day while this son was eating, Sugunanandan knocked the plate from his hands and scolded him. On another day, the villagers abused and threatened him, obstructing his path. Even then, there was not an iota of difference in his attitude. There was only one thought: 'Amma, Amma.' However much his family opposed him, he would not stop coming to the ashram. Sometimes after leaving here for his house, he would immediately return to the ashram on the next bus from a bus stop midway without even going home.

"In the earlier days during Devi Bhava darshan, a begging bowl was kept nearby. The scriptures say, 'One should live renouncing shame and pride.' The begging bowl could be seen only if one looked very carefully. Amma was determined to not ask anything from anyone. No one should think that Amma was sitting for money. The money which was placed in the begging bowl was only sufficient for the needs of the temple. Since Amma did not have any other money to take care of the children who came to the ashram, she would go to the neighbouring houses and beg. Whatever she received she would use to feed the children and herself.

"When Nealu started living here, he said that he would bring whatever was necessary for the ashram, but Amma wouldn't agree. Again Amma went on begging. Amma did not accept his money until Nealu gave his word that he would love everyone equally. Amma agreed only when he looked upon the ashram and the other children as his own.

"The children began staying in the ashram when there were no means for even one meal a day. Still, they didn't feel any difficulty. Without having a place to sleep at night, they would sleep in the coconut groves till daybreak. These children grew up undergoing that much suffering.

"Amritatma had the attitude that Amma was his biological mother. He never had the feeling that this was an ashram or that Amma was his Guru. Rather, he felt this to be his house. He would show as much freedom towards Amma as he would have shown to his biological mother. However severely she would scold him, there was no change in his attitude. When that attitude came, Amma's tests also started. Amma sent several women to him to talk to him. Then, Amma would observe his mind. She should know whether he would become fascinated or moved in those situations, shouldn't she? But he would come and openly tell Amma anything that was told by anyone, whatsoever it was. No fascination was seen in him.

"One day, he wrote, 'I am Amma's slave.' Without knowing this, Amma went to him and said, "Son, Amma has a wish. There is suffering and poverty in our ashram, is there not? Four or five children want to stay here as brahmacharis. They have come for the good of the world, haven't they? Therefore, you should go to the Persian Gulf. You should bear this sacrifice for Amma. If you get a job, you would get at least two or three thousand rupees. Then Amma can raise the brahmacharis." Suddenly, his mood changed and he thought, 'Is it for this I came here, resigning the job which I had? I came

The Vows of Renunciation

to become a sannyasi. Is it not Amma who said that God will protect one if everything is surrendered? Now you say that I must go to Persia?' Actually Amma was testing him. Amma told him, 'Son, what did you write just a few minutes ago? If you have that much dedication, you will not even think twice when Amma says a word. You have not reached that stage to talk about that much surrender. If you had complete surrender, you would have gotten ready to go the moment that Amma had asked you to go. That is the dedication of a Guru-disciple relationship. What you wrote just now has become vain words, has it not? Son, it should be with utmost attention that you say and write each word.'

"One day, having returned after completing his philosophy exams, that son was thinking, 'Is God not within us? Then why should we do sadhana?' Sitting alone, he was thinking philosophically. Amma understood his mentality and sent a letter to him saying, 'Darling son, at the bottom of this letter, Amma has written the word "sugar." Son, you should inform Amma if you get sweetness from licking the word on the paper.' He wondered, 'Would I get sweetness if I were to lick the word "sugar"? Why did Amma write such a letter to me?' Then Amma went to him and said, 'Son, you say that you are Brahman and that God is within. If you say this into a tape recorder and press the play button, it will also say, "I am Brahman." What difference is there between you and the tape recorder? It is not enough to merely say what you have learned. The sweetness of sugar must be experienced; it is not something that can be verbalized. God is experience. At present we are only a seed, not a tree.'

"From the day he came here until last night, every day has been a day of testing for Amritatma. Because of the Lord's grace he came out successful. He has been punished even for silly things. Several times Amma made him go round the ashram having tied a towel over his eyes to shame him. However much a mother scolds the child, the child will tightly catch hold of the mother. Leaving the mother, where else could the child go? There is no other world for the child if bereft of the mother. The more she pushes away the child, the tighter he will hold onto her. Seeing that, the mother will take the child and sing a lullaby, putting him on her shoulder. This is the Guru-disciple relationship.

"Amma would scold Amritatma severely and accuse him of mistakes which he had not made. Without any reason, Amma would even push him. But that son would sit silently without uttering even a word. He would not even move from the place where he was sitting or standing. Finally Amma would ask, 'Son, why are you sitting unmoved without uttering even a word?' Then he would say, 'My Amma can never get angry with me nor can she dislike me. You are my own and I am yours. This is a blessing, your grace to remove my ego. Amma, please bless me always like this.'

"Amma knows that it is not good to praise someone in front of him. It will inflate his ego. But Amma does not have that fear in Amritatma's case. If it happens, Amma is always near to crush it. He knows that. Because of that, Amma would like to say a few more things about him.

"Many times he told Amma certain things which were going to happen. Once on our way back from Madras in the ashram van, Amritatma suddenly told Amma, 'Amma, the wheel of the van is going to fall off. Ask Pai to stop the van.' Amma suddenly repeated this loudly. Pai replied that he would stop the van at the next shady spot. A split second later, one of the wheels fell off. The van bounced violently off the road before Pai could get control. It got bogged down in the sand and wedged against a milestone post. Without the sand and the post the van would surely have tipped over into the ditch on the side of the road. Fortunately nothing serious happened.

"Children, as you all know, it was Amritatma who tuned many of the songs sung here and has also written a few. Also, without asking Amma first, he would never do even the most insignificant things, such as cutting his hair or buying a new pair of sandals. Sometimes when he asked permission for something, Amma wouldn't say anything. If he didn't get an answer from Amma, Amritatma would wait until he got permission. Once, he lost his shoes and whenever he asked permission to buy a new pair, Amma would keep silent. Six months passed and still he walked barefoot. Then, one day Amma gave permission. The Guru will go on observing the disciple while he scolds or accuses him of things which he has or has not done. In the light of these experiences, Amma has the conviction that he will succeed.

"Now that he has been given sannyasa, he has become the son of the world. Hereafter, he is not my son. Today the Lord has given me the good fortune to dedicate one son to the world. At this moment, Amma remembers his father and mother and salutes them also. Children, all of you pray for this son. Pray for him to gain strength. From now onwards, he is not Amritatma Chaitanya, but Amritaswarupananda Puri. Amma (who is not herself a sannyasini) has not gone against the traditional scriptural injunctions by giving him sannyasa. It is in the "Puri" order that sannyasa was given to him (by another sannyasi). Many have asked Amma if it would not have been enough if she had given sannyasa to him? But Amma would never cause a disturbance to the tradition of the ancient sages. Amma will not act against the tradition. Amma had a desire that a humble devotee should give the ochre cloth to Amritatma. Otherwise the ego "I am Brahman, I am Perfect," will develop in him. Such thoughts will not be there if it is a devotee who gives the cloth, is it not so? Amma wanted to give sannyasa through a swami from the Ramakrishna Order. Amma had said long before that a swami from that order who is a devotee will come here when it is time. It was at that time that Swami Dhruvananda came. His Guru was one among Sri Ramakrishna's direct disciples. He came and did the fire ceremony.

"Yesterday, this son performed all the funeral rites both for himself and his relatives. He took leave of his father and mother. He did all the rites that are performed when one dies. All forms of bondage were given up. Hereafter, he is your son, the son of the world. All the duties that one has towards trees, creepers, plants, animals, birds, and all other creatures were eliminated. He performed the fire ceremony praying, 'Make me introverted, lead me to effulgence, spiritual splendour, brilliance, lead me to the Light,' and accepted ochre cloth as a symbol of sacrificing even his own body to the fire. The name Amritaswarupananda was also given. Thus, today is a good day, children. All of you pray, 'Grant this son strength to give peace and tranquillity to everyone in this world. Make him a benefactor of the world.'

"Even a sannyasi's breath should be for the good of others. It is said that he should not even breathe for his own comfort. The whole body has been sacrificed in the Fire of Knowledge. Ochre is the colour of fire. Now he is of the nature of the Self. We are all that eternal Self. He should worship everyone seeing them as Devi or the form of God. It is through human beings that God should be served. Now he doesn't have a particular God. That son should serve the people seeing them as God. His remaining life is to serve them. That is the action that he should do hereafter, to live dedicating his life to them who are verily the forms of God. This son doesn't have a realization or penance higher than that. All that is over. Serve everyone seeing them as God. The duty towards God is compassion towards the poor and needy. Other than that, however much penance you do, there is no benefit. Perfection can be gained only through those actions performed while thinking of God.

"Permission to leave the country cannot be gained without a passport. This passport of Realization should be gained through service. Nothing can be gained without a passport. Now Amma has given more importance to service. With each breath you children have the thought, 'Amma, Amma.' Because of that, Amma has the conviction that you can serve everyone seeing them as God. Children, all of you now pray two minutes for this son. Now he is not a son, but Swami Amritaswarupananda. O God, let him not become a malefactor for anyone in this world. Let him not bring any insult to the great sannyasa tradition. May he have the mental equipoise to see everyone as God and serve them selflessly."

CHAPTER 13

"I Am Always With You"

WHEN TALK OF AMMA'S GOING around the world for the third time had come up, I was of two minds. On the one hand, I didn't like leaving India, and on the other hand, I didn't like being away from Amma for three months continuously. I asked Amma what to do. She told me that since I had applied for Indian citizenship, it was better that I was in India in case any inquiries came from the Indian government. So I decided to stay, and as Amma had hinted, a letter did come from the government asking for some clarification about my previous activities. During that time, I went to the orphanage several times to see how the work was going on. One of the brahmacharis there gave a talk to the children and told a story about some prison inmates. He mentioned the kind of food that the prisoners were given, which was barely cooked flour dough. Hearing this, one of the boys stood up and said, "Swami, that's not just a story.

Before Amma took over this orphanage, we were given the same kind of food for many years. As a result, most of us were suffering from stomach aches and indigestion all the time. Now, for the first time in our lives, we are having good food and a decent place to live." I was very moved to hear the child's words and felt this was reason enough to have taken the orphanage under Amma's care.

The next year, I decided that I would prefer to go with Amma on the tour, rather than stay behind; yet financially it did not seem possible. I was no longer needed on the tour and could not expect the ashram to pay for my ticket, and my physical mother would probably not sponsor my trip as I would not be able to spend any time with her. However, about two months before the 1990 tour, I suddenly herniated a disc in my spine. The doctors recommended complete rest. When the devotees in the ashram in America heard about my condition, they suggested that I go to America for treatment, and Amma also felt that was for the best. My mother offered to buy my ticket. So, after resting for one month, I was sent to San Francisco. Various doctors examined me and decided that an operation might relieve some of the pain. I wanted to wait until Amma's arrival, so I did not have the operation until the beginning of June. However, the

Mata Amritanandamayi Center in San Ramon, California, USA

operation did not give me much relief. Nevertheless, I accompanied Amma on the tour all the way to Boston. At that point, she asked me to stay behind at the American ashram for as long as I could, teaching classes on the Indian scriptures and giving *satsangs* about her teachings. She felt that some spiritual support was needed for the residents there. When I asked her for how long I should stay, she replied, "As long as you can."

Amma left for London and I returned to San Francisco. On the way back, all the lights on the plane started to flash on and off, and the air vents started to blow out air uncontrollably. This lasted for one hour, and it seemed that the electrical system was malfunctioning. "Well, Amma," I thought, "is this going to be the end of the show now, away from you? Was it for this that you have left me here?" I then closed my eyes and repeated my mantra, trying to surrender to the Will of God. But by the time we reached San Francisco, the problem corrected itself.

I stayed at the ashram until Amma's return in May of the next year, giving classes, Saturday satsangs, working on the quarterly magazine, pre-tour work and meeting devotees. I was kept continuously engaged from morning until night. So much so, I did not feel Amma's absence very much since I was engaged in serving her. I have always found over the years that even though being with Amma physically is a tremendous aid to concentration and purity of mind, serving her in some way or other also gives me a lot of peace and happiness.

Many of us do spiritual practices but don't seem to make much progress even after a long time. It may not be obvious to us why this is so. We seem to be so sincere. A conversation between Amma and a young man visiting the California ashram during Amma's fifth world tour is very revealing in this regard.

The young man asked, "It is said that a spiritual aspirant should strictly observe certain rules and regulations as laid down in the scriptures. Are they really compulsory?"

Amma replied, "At present, we are subject to the laws of Nature and therefore we have to observe the rules if we want to make spiritual progress. This is unavoidable until we reach a certain stage in our sadhana. In the state where Nature has become our servant, rules are not necessary, for there will be no loss of spiritual energy, even if we do not follow them. But until then, they are necessary.

"After sowing a seed in the soil, we cover it with netting to protect it from birds; otherwise, the seeds will be eaten or the shoots will be destroyed and nothing will grow. Once the seed has become a big tree, it will be capable of giving protection to birds, human beings and even elephants. Similarly, once we have discovered the strength that is latent within ourselves, rules, which serve to protect us will no longer be necessary.

"Are regularity and steadiness in practice necessary for this to happen?" asked the boy.

"Yes, we should love regularity and steadiness as much as we love God. One who loves God will love discipline also, but of the two we should love discipline and regularity first," answered Amma.

"Those who have a habit of drinking tea or coffee at a fixed hour become restless or get a headache if they do not get it at the usual time. Those who are addicted to drugs become agonized if they miss their accustomed dose. Their habit reminds them each day at the same hour to repeat the same action. Likewise, if we practice regularity in any action, a habit will be formed. In the case of sadhana, this will be of benefit to us, for we will be reminded to do sadhana at the proper time.

The young man said, "I do a sadhana, but I do not see any benefit."

Looking at him with a compassionate smile on her face, Amma asked him, "Son, you often lose your temper, don't you?"

"Yes," he retorted, "but so what? What is the connection between my getting angry and my sadhana?"

"If a person does sadhana without giving up pride and anger," Amma responded, "he will not be able to derive any benefit from it. Son, you collect a little sugar on one side and then let the ants in on the other. What is earned by you through sadhana is wasted through your anger. However, you are unaware of that loss. If we press the switch of a flashlight ten times, the charge in the battery will go down. Similarly, when we get angry, all our energy is lost through the eyes, ears, nose, mouth and all the pores of the skin. Due to pride and anger, our energy is dissipated. But if we keep our mind under control, what we have earned will remain with us."

"Are those who get angry unable to experience the bliss attainable through sadhana?" asked the young man.

Amma replied, "My child, imagine that we are drawing water from a well using a bucket that has many holes. By the time the bucket reaches the top of the well, there will be no more water in it, for the water has all gone out through the holes. Son, your sadhana is like this. If sadhana is done with the mind full of desires and anger, whatever is gained is continually lost. That is why we are not able to realize the benefit, experience the bliss, or even understand the greatness of sadhana. Therefore, you should, first of all, sit in a lonely place to calm down your mind and then do your spiritual practice. Stay far away from anger and desires; then you can certainly realize the source of boundless energy and bliss."

Shortly after Amma's return from the eighth world tour in August 1994, Amma decided to continue the tradition of giving sannyasa to her disciples. Six men and two women received the ochre cloth. They were Ramakrishna (Swami Ramakrishnananda), Rao (Swami Amritatmananda), Sreekumar (Swami Purnamritananda), Venu (Swami Pranavamritananda), Satyatma (Swami Amritageetananda), Leela (Swamini Atmaprana) and Gayatri (Swamini Amritaprana). The atmosphere in the ashram had certainly changed from the early days. Although it was still a big family, there was much more seriousness about spiritual life now. The swamis were put in charge of different branch ashrams and the ashram residents were expected to maintain high standards of spiritual discipline. Regular classes were conducted in the Vedanta philosophy and many were initiated into the vows of *brahmacharya* (celibate student life). From the three or four of us who used to live with Amma, the ashram had expanded to nearly four hundred permanent residents.

Real ashrams come up like this. They are not built with a plan. They "happen" around a Mahatma. They are the real holy places on earth. The vibrations of the sage who lives at the center of it all pervade the atmosphere there. Add to this the good vibrations of all the devotees and disciples who are doing sadhana and you have a powerful environment for leading a life of spirituality. Even in Amma's physical absence, one can feel the intense peace of the atmosphere in her ashram in Kerala. Those vibrations will never dissipate as long as there are aspirants striving for God in that place. This is how holy places come into being.

After Amma had given sannyasa to these disciples, she talked to me, and asked if I would also accept the same. Who was I to decide such a thing? Although I had been leading a life of renunciation for the past twenty-six years, I had no intention of becoming a sannyasi. My only wish was to realize God. Yet, perhaps for the good of the world and to increase my own detachment, Amma wanted me to accept the ochre cloth. It was obvious from her question that she wanted me to do so. I unhesitatingly said "Yes." She said that the next time I visited India, she would arrange the ceremony, as I was still in America at that time.

Amma had told me that I should return to India once every two years. This was not merely for the pleasure of being in the ashram. She felt that it was necessary for my purity of mind that I "charge my batteries" now and then. Although the ashram in America had become a holy place in itself and was full of the flavour of India's spiritual culture, I also felt that I had to regularly live in the Indian atmosphere. The lack of a common tradition in America makes spiritual life very difficult to maintain, for the ideals of Western society are based not on self-control, right action and devotion to God, but rather on comfort, pleasure and the supremacy of the human intellect. If one were to go into a room where charcoal is stored while wearing white clothes, one cannot help getting soiled, however so slightly it may be. Having lived in the traditional culture of India for more than half my life, I found it conducive for my spiritual progress. After staying in America on a more or less permanent basis, I also understood the wisdom of regularly visiting India and staying there for some time.

The sannyasa ceremony was performed at the end of August 1995. The first day was the ceremony of shaving the head and performing one's own funeral rites by the ocean side. The next morning, the fire ceremony started by three a.m. It was led by Swami Amritaswarupananda. Due to continuing physical problems with my back and digestive system, I was undergoing a lot of suffering. I was simply unable to sit so many hours. Yet, I decided, as I had done many other times in my life, that I would "do or die."

Amma came to the fire ceremony at about six o'clock. Although I was not "making faces," she could immediately tell that I was in a lot a pain. Turning towards me, she said, "It will only be another hour." There were five of us and so it took quite a while. It was more like two or three hours before the ceremony completed. At last, Amma gave us our new ochre robes, blessed us and sent us to the ocean to complete the ceremony there. After returning to the ashram, we begged our food from the devotees and then spent some time with Amma again. Looking at me, she smiled and said, "Did you die? Poor boy!" "No, Amma," I replied. "But a great deal of my past bad karma has been burnt away by today's ordeal." Hearing this, Amma laughed. I wish that I could have sat there blissfully like the others, but at least I was not upset by the pain I had to go through. I took it as another opportunity to practice detachment from the body. Amma gave me the name of Swami Paramatmananda. The others who received sannyasa that day were Unnikrishnan (Swami Turiyamritananda), Damu (Swami Prajnanamritananda),

Amma with Swami Paramatmananda
after the sannyasa initiation ceremony

Unnikrishnadas (Swami Jnanamritananda) and Saumya (Swamini Krishnamrita Prana).

Everyday I used to stroll near Amma's room, as that was the most peaceful place in the ashram. Most of the other areas were usually full of people, but around Amma's room it was generally kept empty in order not to disturb Amma too much. As I was walking back and forth in a meditative mood, Amma came down the stairs on her way to the evening singing and Devi Bhava. I was about a hundred feet away from Amma when I spotted her. Generally she walks very fast while on the way to a place. This time she stopped and looked at me. Although I had no intention of going near her, knowing that she was in a hurry, I felt an intense longing to rush to her, my heart full of love towards her. She just stood there waiting. I practically ran and fell at her feet. She smiled and said, "Son, why don't you sing tonight during the darshan?" "All right, Amma," I replied. In fact, I had just been thinking about the fact that I had not been able to sing during the darshan because there were so many others that wanted to. I felt that it would be selfish on my part to take away their chance of singing in front of Amma. The powerful fact of Amma's omniscience and power to attract me to her once again impressed itself upon my mind.

I Am Always With You

Soon after this, Amma started to ask me when I would be returning to America. I had only been in India for a few weeks! What was the hurry? I hinted at the same to Amma without showing any disrespect. "All right, you go when you feel like it," she said. But over the next three weeks she asked me again and again when I was going. It did not take much to understand that my work lay in America. It seemed that Amma wanted me to entirely forget my own happiness, and to serve without any selfishness at all.

I went to her room one morning to spend a little time in her presence. She started to discuss my return to America, at which point I said, "Amma, I have spent nearly six years away from you. How is it that I must live twelve thousand miles away from you, the Divine Mother Herself, while you enact your divine drama here? And now I have to go again after such a short stay. Is this my future?"

Looking at me intently but with loving grace shining in her eyes, Amma said, "Son, you came to me for God-Realization. Shouldn't one keep one's mind in God, wherever one may be in this world? Never think that Amma's grace is not with you. You are never away from Amma. Always remember that wherever you may go in this universe, now or after death, Amma will be by your side forever."

Hearing Amma's words, my heart filled with emotion at the thought of her eternal love and divinity. I could say nothing more. Bowing down to her feet, I left, sad at the thought of the impending physical separation, but filled with the faith that Amma would be with me always, and at the right time, would awaken me from the dark nightmare of birth, death and rebirth into the brilliant sunshine of Self-knowledge.